Hawaii

Berlitz®
Hawaii

Text by J.D. Brown and Margaret Backenheimer
Edited by Media Content Marketing, Inc.
Photography: J.D. Brown
Cover photograph: © J. Silver/SuperStock
Layout: Media Content Marketing, Inc.
Cartography by Raffaele De Gennaro
Managing Editor: Tony Halliday

Eleventh Edition 2002 (Reprinted 2004)

CONTACTING THE EDITORS

Every effort has been made to provide accurate information in this publication, but changes are inevitable. The publisher cannot be responsible for any resulting loss, inconvenience or injury. We would appreciate it if readers would call our attention to any errors or outdated information by contacting Berlitz Publishing, PO Box 7910, London SE1 1WE, England. Fax: (44) 20 7403 0290;
e-mail: berlitz@apaguide.co.uk; www.berlitzpublishing.com

040/311 RP

CONTENTS

● A  in the text denotes a highly recommended sight

Hawaii

HAWAII AND THE HAWAIIANS

Hawaii, America's 50th state, stands a world apart from the US mainland. Not only are its geography, history, and culture exotic and unique, but Hawaii also possesses an unfair measure of what people seek when they travel, from golf greens and gardens to coral reefs and beach umbrellas. There's even a very active volcano. Hawaii, quite simply, is America's island paradise – albeit a paradise with American characteristics.

Democracy rules in Hawaii: There is something special for everyone who visits. The islands are endlessly young, beautiful, and athletic (endowed with plenty of surf, an abundance of coconut palms and lush ferns, and weather that's warm enough year-round for swimwear and sandals).

The cultural mix and remoteness of Hawaii have created a unique society, yet one that is not baffling or alien. Hawaii is far from home, but familiar at the same time. The residents constitute one of the world's true melting pots. If any place can claim to be the meeting place of East and West, it is Hawaii, where peoples from both sides of the Pacific have blended into a unique society.

Above all, the Hawaiian Islands are blessed with an abundance of fine tourist attractions and facilities. These days, Hawaii is best known as an island resort, a getaway for honeymooners, vacationers, surfers, and other outdoor enthusiasts, most of whom hail from America, Europe, or Japan. You can find some of the world's best beaches here, watch pods of migrating whales from your beach chair, snorkel and dive at nearby coral reefs, visit an active volcano where lava flows daily to the sea, and spend your nights at some of the most impressive resorts ever built.

To do all of this, you'll have to journey far across the sea. Consisting of six main islands, the Hawaiian archipelago is located 2,350 miles (3,800 km) west of California, so far across the Pacific Ocean from North America and from Asia that it ranks as one of the world's most far-flung outposts. Western explorers didn't stumble upon its pristine beaches until 1778.

Hawaii Tidbits

Hawaii is the most isolated island group in the world, 2,350 miles from California, 3,850 miles from Japan.

Honolulu is closer to Tokyo than to New York City.

Iolani Palace in Honolulu is the only royal palace in the US – and the first palace in the world to install flush toilets.

Billboards are banned in Hawaii; commercial signs are restricted to the relevant business's property.

The steel guitar was invented in Hawaii, but the ukulele (a Hawaiian word meaning "jumping flea") was imported by the Portuguese.

Hawaii has the largest dormant volcano in the world (Haleakala, on Maui) and the only currently active lava cone in the US (Kilauea, on the Big Island).

Hawaii is the most racially and ethnically diverse state in the US.

Many of the 100,000 wild pigs in Hawaii are descended from those the early Polynesians brought to the islands in canoes.

The Parker Ranch on the Big Island is the second largest cattle ranch in the US.

You can ski and snorkel on the same day on the Big Island (but ski first to avoid the "bends").

Hawaii has the highest per capita consumption of watermelons in the US.

The southernmost tip of the US is on the Big Island at Ka Lae.

All the islands were formed by volcanoes; currently the undersea volcano of Loihi is rising and may one day become Hawaii's most southern island.

Youngsters survey the surf during yet another beautiful day at Punaluu Beach, on the Big Island.

Before then, and for long afterwards, it was a Polynesian kingdom, and the native Hawaiian people have left an indelible mark on the culture of their islands. Whalers and missionaries built towns and churches on Hawaii's shores in the 19th century; sugar and pineapple plantations followed, creating a trading empire; and early travelers, from Mark Twain to the movie stars of the 1920s and 1930s, arriving on steamers and cruise ships, created a mystique about Hawaii that persists to this day.

The emergence of mass travel by air propelled the islands to preeminence as a tropical destination. Hawaii obliged, turning Waikiki into a major resort strip and the neighboring islands into the setting for some of the world's grandest resorts. When the Mauna Kea, the pet project of Laurance Rockefeller, opened in 1965 on the Big Island of Hawaii, it was hailed as the best beach resort in the world. A rash of condos and championship golf courses followed.

Hula, originally performed only by men, is an integral part of Hawaiian culture.

While the resorts are splendid getaways, it is nature herself that overwhelms the senses in Hawaii. The big population of coconut palms, the magnificent lushness of fern forests, the sheer heights of volcanic peaks, the expanse of dark lava fields, and the proliferation of perfect white sand beaches impart to Hawaii the appearance of a world still fresh from creation. The days are long and lazy, the warm air fragrant, the nights often clear and intensely starry. (Hawaii's remoteness, combined with the extraordinary height of its volcanic peaks, has made these islands the location of some of the world's top astronomical observatories.) The island chain stretches in a 1,500-mile (2,413-km) arc as far north as Midway Atoll, but the main islands are all within a few minutes' hop by plane. If one island becomes too dull or too crowded for your taste, another isle is always near at hand, perhaps a far less crowded one with plenty of new attractions (like a coast of sheer seacliffs accessible only by foot or sea).

Yet Hawaii is not simply an island chain for tourists. While there are clusters of beach hotels and resort strips reminiscent of those in the Caribbean, Cancun, or Monaco, each of the Hawaiian islands has kept much of its own beauty and character. Rent a car (as most island visitors do) and you can discover historic towns off the beaten track, local beaches and gardens, mountain trails, and prehistoric valleys miles from the myriad of shopping streets and condos. One of Hawaii's charms is that it is big enough to offer a variety of treasures, and Hawaii's variety extends to its individual isles: They are all compellingly different, each with its own version of an island paradise.

The island of Oahu is Hawaii's population center, home of the capital, Honolulu (the state's only large city), and site of its most famous beach, Waikiki. Along Waikiki, running to picturesque Diamond Head (an extinct volcanic cone), is an array of historic and towering modern beach hotels, the primary stop for most tourists. Parallel to the beach, which is always full of surfers and tanners, is Hawaii's biggest shopping street, with an intriguing collection of boutiques, restaurants, alfresco cafés, markets, plazas, and nightclubs. This is Hawaii's resort central, a fine introduction to what Hawaii offers the vacationer.

Honolulu has an Old Waikiki as well, with historic hotels and a statue commemorating Hawaii's legendary surfer and

Hula

There's nothing lascivious about the hula. In fact, hula kahiko, or the ancient hula, was a sacred part of Hawaiian religion, originally performed by men only. By the time the missionaries arrived in 1820, both men and women practiced the hula, the men in loincloths and the women topless but in tapa or ti-leaf skirts. Shocked by what they perceived as a vulgar display, the missionaries worked to ban the hula. When King Kalakaua came to power in 1874, however, he revived the practice. Today he is honored at the Merrie Monarch Festival in Hilo every April, when both hula kahiko (ancient hula, done to the beat of a drum) and hula auwana (modern hula, done to music) are celebrated. In fact, hula halaus (schools or groups) are found all over Hawaii and in places as far away as Sweden. In Hawaii, tourists will have little trouble finding a hula performance or lesson. Hula groups perform regularly at the Kodak Hula Show in the Waikiki Shell (Tuesday, Wednesday, Thursday, 10am) and at Kuhio Beach Stage in Waikiki (every day, 6:30pm).

Olympic swimming champion, Duke Kahanamoku. Downtown Honolulu provides even more visible chapters of the islands' legacy, including a colorful Chinatown, a maritime museum recounting the whaling tradition, the coral church and mission houses established by the first missionaries, the Bishop Museum (Hawaii's premier collection of native and Polynesian artifacts), and America's only royal palace, Iolani, where the last king and queen of Hawaii ruled.

Honolulu is also the location of Pearl Harbor, the enormous naval base that was devastated in the surprise attack by Japan on 7 December 1941; the daily tours of the USS Arizona Memorial are moving and memorable. While Honolulu has become Hawaii's urban tourist center, the rest of Oahu offers real escapes, with garden estates, sugar and pineapple plantations, and beaches dotted with surfing towns.

The island of Maui is less populated than Oahu. The resort developments on the west shore, at Kaanapali and Wailea, are a little less frenzied than those on Waikiki, and Maui has more intimate attractions, such as the whaling village of Lahaina and a plethora of outdoor attractions. Highlights include the dormant crater atop Haleakala (10,023 ft/3,055 m) and the moss-covered Iao Valley. The east side of the island is legendary for the twisting, narrow road to Hana, with its scores of one-lane bridges, and pools and forests that are positively prehistoric.

The sparsely populated Big Island of Hawaii, by far the largest and most southerly isle, boasts a handful of Hawaii's most awesome and relaxing resort hotels, built on a vast landscape of black lava fields created by the eruptions of its giant volcanoes. From the coffee plantations of Kona and the snorkeling and diving hotspot of Molokini to the ranges of Parker Ranch and the native sanctuary of Puuhonua O Honaunau "City of Refuge," the Big Island offers sharp contrasts to its more developed neighbors. The center is dominated by Hawaii

Volcanoes National Park, where Mauna Loa (13,670ft/ 4,206m) still sends rivers of fresh lava to the sea.

Kauai, the oldest and most northerly of Hawaii's main islands, is by comparison a true garden of Eden. Wet and lush, carpeted in flowers and trees, Kauai was the setting for scenes in the movie *South Pacific*. There are two scenic wonders here, Waimea Canyon, also dubbed the

For many visitors, Hawaii is synonymous with surfing.

"Grand Canyon of the Pacific" by Mark Twain and the Na Pali Coast, a roadless challenge for hikers along sheer ocean cliffs. Visitors find Kauai less spoiled than Oahu, Maui, or the Big Island, a botanical isle that captures the essence of Hawaiian hospitality and tradition.

Two even less developed islands have begun to attract visitors to Hawaii. The island of Molokai, crossed by a single, winding road, is celebrated as the location of a leper colony founded by Father Damien. Visitors can descend the nearly impassable cliffs to this colony, still functioning as a refuge for those with Hansen's disease, via a mule train (there is no road). Molokai's main resort is a large ranch, now a haven for horseback riders and trail bikers. Still smaller is Lanai, until recently a pineapple plantation and company island owned by Dole, now a getaway featuring two upscale resorts and the remains of the company town.

Whatever paradise one seeks, from big tropical resorts to tiny, tradition-bound hideaways, the islands of Hawaii provide a perfect escape.

A BRIEF HISTORY

The history of Hawaii reads like the story of a mythical kingdom. The first wave of Polynesian settlers crossed the equator and arrived from the Marquesas in the South Pacific perhaps as early as A.D. 400. These immigrant voyages were breathtaking and treacherous, requiring the crossing of 2,500 miles (4,000 km) of open seas aboard dugout catamarans and outrigger canoes. Seeking to escape domestic turmoil, they navigated by stars and literally reading the ocean and its contours. Their destination was even more resplendent with forests than the paradise we see today, and hoary bats and monk seals were the only mammals in residence.

The first Polynesian settlers, however, brought much of what they needed to eke out a living, from pigs and chickens to bananas and *taro*, the root crop that would sustain them. Paddies of taro are to this day a signature crop in rural Hawaii.

A second wave of Polynesian immigrants from Tahiti arrived centuries later. By A.D. 1300 they had erased the vestiges of a Marquesan outpost and developed a Hawaiian society of their own. Rival chiefs ruled each island; fish farms and temples were laid out; and tribal and inter-island warfare was common. The chiefs governed their feudal domains by force, ritual, and taboo. The system of taboo *(kapu)* gave society its laws and the people a complex moral code. To fend off natural and cosmic catastrophes, the rituals of human sacrifice came into play, intended to placate the more violent of the local gods, such as those of the volcanoes and typhoons.

While such island societies might seem less than Edenic, the early Hawaiians led a pleasurable life, singing their own histories to the beat of gourds, riding the waves on long wooden surfboards, and developing an elaborate, graceful form of story-dance, the *hula*.

Captains and Kings

The first Westerner to reach Hawaii was Captain James Cook, whose mission was to discover the mythic Northwest Passage linking the Atlantic and Pacific oceans. He, too, had set out from Tahiti when he came upon the Hawaiian Islands. The year was 1778; his landfall was the northerly island of Kauai; and the name he gave his new discovery was the Sandwich Islands (after the Lord of the Admiralty, the Earl of Sandwich). The name did not stick, and had Captain Cook known his fate, he would not have stuck around either. The natives seemed friendly enough, rowing out to greet Cook's ships, which received

Captain Cook still stands in Waimea, harking back to his Hawaiian arrival in 1778.

much-needed provisions in exchange for fastenings and other trinkets. When Cook later tied up on the Big Island of Hawaii, at Kealakekua Bay, he was hailed as the god Lono and feasted on a grand scale. But returning later to regroup after being slapped by an angry storm, a dispute arose over stolen property. Cook took a chief hostage, and in turn he was ritualistically hacked to pieces.

Cook's cohorts had opened fire, to no avail. Among those wounded that day was the young man who would soon unite the Hawaiian kingdom for the first time in its long history. Known as Kamehameha the Great, he considered the unification of Hawaii his divine fate, one which he was to fulfill before he turned 30. He did so with the help of a foreign navy vessel. After Cook's voyage, a small but steady flow of American and European vessels, already engaged in the China trade, started to use Hawaii as a convenient, much-needed stopover. The warring chiefs demanded guns in exchange for food. Kamehameha, as chief of the Big Island, not only got his share of guns, but finally captured a cannon and ship. Maui fell first, followed by Oahu, Lanai, and Molokai. Kauai, where Cook had begun his fateful voyage of Hawaiian discovery, became Kamehameha's vassal in 1810.

As the first king of all Hawaii, Kamehameha established a new empire that preserved the old ways, including the rituals performed at the outdoor temples *(heiau),* while creating an overlay of British-style government. A viceroy ruled each island at the King's pleasure. These Western ideas, which seemed to amuse Kamehameha, were introduced by a new friend, another famous English explorer, Captain George Vancouver, who had once served under Captain Cook. The King encouraged the arrival of Westerners, giving land grants to some of his favorite foreigner visitors. Vancouver had left scores of cattle and sheep on the islands to supply passing ships. To round them up, the King brought cowboys from Spain and Mexico, initiating the *paniolo* (Hawaiian cowboy) tradition. Another seafarer, the American John Kendrick, launched the sandalwood trade in 1791, when China had run out of its own supply. By 1825, Hawaii's sandalwood forests had been thoroughly cut away, too, and non-native flora and fauna were imported to fill in, altering the landscape of paradise.

There were other changes, too. Among the commodities exchanged when foreign ships called were Hawaiian women, who

Historical Landmarks

c. A.D. 400 Polynesian voyagers begin to settle the Hawaiian Islands.

c. A.D. 1300 Polynesian chiefs from Tahiti rule the islands.

1778 Captain James Cook "discovers" Hawaii; dies there the next year.

1810 Kamehameha the Great unites Hawaii under its first King.

1819 Kamehameha II succeeds to the throne; dismantles the traditional system of taboos. Whalers make Hawaii a major port.

1820 American missionaries arrive in Honolulu.

1823 Much of the royal court converts to Christianity.

1824 Kamehameha III comes to power.

1840 Establishment of a constitutional monarchy reduces the King's power. Foreign sugar barons gain an upper hand.

1848 Private ownership of land allowed.

1852 Immigrant laborers from Asia begin the transformation of Hawaii's population.

1874 David Kalakaua elected as constitutional monarch. Whaling industry declines.

1882 The King rules from Iolani, the only royal palace on US soil.

1891 Queen Liliuokalani succeeds her brother, resists US annexation and foreign influence.

1893 The Queen is overthrown by plantation owners.

1894 Sanford Dole becomes president of new Hawaii Republic.

1898 Hawaii annexed by US. Sanford Dole becomes first US Territorial governor.

1912 Hawaii's premier surfer, Duke Kahanamoku, wins Olympic gold medal in swimming.

1936 Commercial air service from San Francisco inaugurated.

1941 Pearl Harbor bombed by Japan; US enters World War II.

1959 Hawaii becomes the 50th US state.

1983 Kilauea volcano begins decades of eruptions, lava flows.

1990 Hawaii reaches tourism peak; 7 million visitors annually. Sugar and pineapple industries reduced.

2000 Revival of native culture spurs rights movements.

2002 Tourism declines after New York's September 11 attacks.

King Kamehameha the Great presides over historic Central Honolulu.

soon gained a measure of economic independence through prostitution and other endeavors involving outsiders. Foreign ships carried new diseases to the islands as well. Measles, cholera, and syphilis soon riddled the population, which was cut in half over just a few decades. By the time the first great king of Hawaii died, in 1819, the underpinnings of native society were disintegrating.

Missionaries, Whales and Sugarcane

The year of 1820 was a pivotal one in the story of the Kingdom of Hawaii. It was the year the first missionaries arrived from America. But more immediately, it was when the *kapu* system of taboos broke down completely under the leadership of young King Kamehameha II (the first king's son, Liholiho) and the regent, Kaahumanu (the favorite of the 21 wives of the first king). Hawaii's royalty resisted replacing the old religious system with newly-arrived Christianity until Kaahumanu was nursed back to health and converted by the wife of one of the first missionaries, Hiram Bingham.

Regent Kaahumanu attended church and the mission schools (which you can still visit in Honolulu) and burned images of

Our Lady of Sorrows Church, one of five founded on Molokai by Father Damien, friend to the lepers.

the old Hawaiian gods, while Kamehameha II entertained lavishly in the company of his wives. In 1824, the King decided to travel abroad, but immediately upon disembarking in England he contacted measles, dying in London.

Many in the church and among the native population viewed the King's overseas death as a judgement. The regent Kaahumanu, ruling in the name of her young charge, Kamehameha III, seized the opportunity and followed many of the strictures favored by the Calvinist Congregationalists, who were modernizing the country through the establishment of schools and the printing of books in the Hawaiian language (which they formulated in a written form for the first time).

Among Kaahumanu's many reforms was the banning of prostitution, a ruling which led to pitched battles in whaling ports such as Lahaina. Alcohol sales, gambling, and dancing were banned for a time in Honolulu. The Calvinistic reforms

Sugar production well made up for the waning of the whaling trade after 1860.

were soon reversed when Kaahumanu died and Kamehameha III ascended to power in 1824.

The new King resumed the ways of the two previous monarchs, abolishing laws against adultery and prostitution and taking up with his half sister; but powerful interests, particularly those of the flourishing foreign business community (which would be increasingly dominated by the descendants of the first missionaries), were intent on usurping the throne, in effect if not in name. The new King was eventually persuaded to issue a decree guaranteeing religious freedom, and the next year, 1840, he established a constitutional monarchy.

The most famous Prime Minister under Hawaii's new political system was an American missionary and physician, Gerrit P. Judd, who served in the post from 1842 to 1854. During this period, foreigners were allowed to buy large parcels of land for the first time (much of it used for the sugarcane plantations), and ties to America, both economic and political, were dramatically tightened, with talk of possibly annexing Hawaii reaching the White House.

However, many Hawaiians were opposed to surrendering their sovereignty. When a new king, Kamehameha IV, ascended to the throne in 1854, Judd was tossed out. The missionary influence waned, and the royal court asserted its power, as well as its love of luxury. The Hawaiian economy was rising, sustained in part by whaling. But the demand for whale oil would decline steeply after 1859, with the discovery of oil in Pennsylvania and the start of the American Civil War in 1860. No matter – Hawaii had a great crop in reserve: sugar. The first refinery appeared in 1849 on Maui. The cane plantations, increasingly in the hands of American tycoons, found a ready market in the US. Duty-free sugar imports from Hawaii were eventually granted by the US, in exchange for rights to a military base at Pearl Harbor in the future.

The growth of the sugar market led to waves of immigration from China (1852), the Azores (1878), and Japan (1885). Native Hawaiians were finding themselves overwhelmed and outnumbered. Disease had lowered the Hawaiian population to just 20 percent of what it was when Captain Cook arrived. The Kamehameha line ended with the death of Kamehameha V,

Lei of the Land

May Day is Lei Day in Hawaii, but then every day is lei day. Not just for tourists, leis are exchanged among friends and family to mark special occasions. Often they are fashioned of flowers strung by hand – each island has its own official flower. Simple plumeria leis are the most common – and perhaps the most sensuous because they bathe the wearer in their heady fragrance. Leis of shells, seeds, braided leaves, and kukui nuts are also popular. Museums feature the beautiful feather leis once worn by the Hawaiian royalty, made of brilliantly colored feathers from exotic birds. In Honolulu, flower leis may be purchased at little shops on Beretania and Maunakea Streets and at the airport. They can sometimes be found at impromptu roadside stands, too, and at outdoor events and festivals, where "aunties" can be seen stringing their fresh creations.

in 1872, and the election first of William Lunalilo, then of David Kalakaua in 1874 as Hawaii's constitutional monarch.

The Merry Monarch

The Hawaiian people loved their King, who was soon dubbed the "Merry Monarch." In 1881, King David Kalakaua launched a world tour, visiting the heads of state in Japan, Thailand, Egypt, and England. The next year, he built himself a palace, Iolani, which can still be toured in Honolulu. He also legalized the hula, Hawaii's traditional dance. But the King's nationalism upset the vested interests of foreigners. Sanford Dole, head of a missionary family, and others led a successful movement to curb Kalakaua's powers. When the King died during a tour of San Francisco, in 1891, he was succeeded by his sister, Liliuokalani, who proved to be an expectedly fierce defender

The mausoleum of King Lunalilo, Hawaii's first elected monarch, stands in downtown Honolulu.

of Hawaiian ways and the monarchy. Dole and others thought it high time for a US coup, and they were able to persuade the US naval forces to assist in deposing the Queen in 1893. When the US refused to annex Hawaii, and instead demanded the re-institution of the Queen, the sugar industry simply declared Hawaii a Republic, with Sanford B. Dole its president. A new US President, McKinley, made annexation official in 1898. In 1900, Hawaii became a US Territory; the first territorial governor was Dole. Queen Liliuokalani lived out her life near Honolulu, quietly and defiantly; she composed songs, including Hawaii's most famous, *Aloha Oe*.

Pineapples and War

The mythical kingdom of Hawaii was now a dream of the past. Political and economic power resided with non-Hawaiians. Dole and other business families were turning vast fields into pineapple plantations and importing new workers to plant and cultivate them. Puerto Ricans began arriving in 1900, followed by Koreans in 1903 and Filipinos from 1907 on. Like the Japanese, Chinese, and Portuguese before them, many of the new peoples would stay on in Hawaii, adding to the ethnic and racial mix that has become a hallmark of the islands. By 1920, the Japanese in Hawaii outnumbered Hawaiians two to one.

Yet Hawaii was still an island paradise in the eyes of travelers, if not in those of its original people. Kilauea volcano on the Big Island had been attracting tourists since the 1860s, but it wasn't until after 1901, with the opening of the Moana Hotel in Waikiki, that organized tourism took hold. Steamships of the Matson Line soon were arriving regularly at Aloha Tower, bearing tourists from San Francisco who had been at sea for five long days. America's rich made up a goodly portion of these early travelers. They arrived with maids and trunks, and often stayed for months. In 1936, Pan American Airways introduced

Casualties of the Japanese attack on Pearl Harbor are remembered at the USS Arizona Memorial.

daily passenger air service from San Francisco. The annual number of visitors had increased to over 30,000 by the time World War II began.

The war broke out in Hawaii as nowhere else in America with the surprise attack on Pearl Harbor (7 December 1941). The US declared war on Japan. Hawaii, as America's western outpost and major Pacific military base, was ruled by martial law. The Waikiki hotels housed soldiers; the white sands were strung with barbed wire; and even the American currency in local circulation was stamped as HAWAII dollars, so that the enemy could not spend it on the world market if the islands fell.

Statehood and Tourism

After the war, sugarcane and pineapple production remained strong for a time, but tourism began its rise to ascendancy. Spurred on by the "Hawaii Calls" live radio program broadcast weekly to the US, Canada, and Australia from Waikiki, millions fell under the spell of a new island paradise of surf and hula aimed at tourists. Trader Vic's opened garish Polynesian-themed restaurants; Arthur Godfrey brought the ukulele to television; Burt Lancaster and Deborah Kerr rolled in the wet sands of Oahu for the film *From Here to Eternity*; and jet air service brought in vacationers by the hundred thousands. The surge was topped off by Hawaii's statehood, on 21 August 1959, but the vision of a mythical kingdom on America's Pacific frontier was still expanding. Hilton built a resort village right on Waikiki Beach; Sheraton and other hotel chains followed. Among the millions of visitors lured there in the 1980s were huge waves of Japanese vacationers, newly rich and ready to spend big bucks in an East-West paradise.

By 1990, Hawaii was welcoming nearly 7 million visitors annually, seven times its own resident population, which is the most ethnically and racially diverse in the US. The same year, the University of Hawaii campus at Manoa became the site of the Center for Cultural and Technical Interchange Between East and West (popularly known as the East West Center), a unique and venerated resource for advanced Pacific Rim studies.

More recently, the overwhelmed native Hawaiian culture underwent a renewal as well. The return and preservation of ancient traditions was a response, in part, to the increasing demand of savvy tourists for a cultural as well as a leisure experience. The other and more important impetus was a growing movement by native Hawaiians to restore the rights stolen from them when the royal monarchy was overthrown. This movement has led to calls for self-determination and increased native sovereignty, even full independence as a new nation for the estimated 250,000 people of Hawaiian ancestry. But perhaps the greatest legacy to travelers today who arrive at the world's premier island beach resort is the warmth, friendliness, and sense of family that Hawaiian culture has created in the land of its rise, fall, and renewal.

WHERE TO GO

With six main islands beckoning, it is not easy to choose a Hawaiian destination. If it is your first trip to the islands, you'll probably want to start in Honolulu, on the island of Oahu, where most of the hotels, most of the people, and many of the best sights are located. If time allows, then take a hop (by air) to one of the neighboring islands, as they present a vivid contrast to busy Honolulu. Return visits will give you time to explore more of the Hawaii beyond Honolulu. Wherever you begin, rent a car; it is the best way to take in the array of attractions on each island.

OAHU

The large majority of Hawaii's residents call Oahu home, most of them residing in and around Honolulu, the state's only metropolis and the center of sun, surf, and shopping. Oahu became Hawaii's political, economic, and tourism capital more than a century ago, primarily because of its good harbor. While Honolulu is Oahu's urban center, home to Waikiki's hotels, condos, shops, and fine beachfront, it also contains many cultural attractions not to be missed, from Iolani Palace and the Mission Houses to the Bishop Museum and a vibrant Chinatown. On the outskirts is Pearl Harbor, where the Arizona Memorial is a poignant reminder of World War II and the military presence that shaped Hawaii.

Beyond the confines of Honolulu, Waikiki, and Pearl Harbor, Oahu offers a sampling of attractions synonymous with "Hawaiian paradise." Driving north up Oahu, one comes across small towns with dazzling beaches, garden estates, old plantations, waterfalls, ancient temples, a Buddhist shrine, a Polynesian cultural center, and misty mountain peaks rising over 4,000 ft (1,220 m). Oahu's North Shore is justly famed

Hawaiian Highlights

Oahu: Waikiki Beach is the tourist center of the islands, worth strolling or playing on; so is the parallel shopping street. Hidden beneath the glitter are veins of the old royal and romantic Waikiki (see page 28).

The Bishop Museum is a repository of Hawaiiana and its Polynesian legacies (see page 36).

The USS Arizona Memorial at Pearl Harbor powerfully evokes the outbreak of World War II in the Pacific (see page 39).

The North Shore combines native Hawaiian culture and natural beauty with the modern charm of surfing villages and beaches (see page 41).

Hanauma Bay, a gorgeous volcanic amphitheater on the shores beyond Diamond Head, draws thousands of snorkelers to its gentle reefs (see page 41).

Maui: The vast Mount Haleakala caldera towers over the island (see page 51).

Lahaina, once the chief whaling port of the Pacific, teems with period architecture and trendy shops (see page 46).

The road to and from Hana goes through the heart of tropical forests and the "real Hawaii" (see page 53).

Hawaii (Big Island): The Kona Coast has superb beaches and the Puuhonua-O-Honaunau "City of Refuge," Hawaii's most striking native temple grounds (see page 62).

Volcanoes National Park has active lava flows flowing to the sea at the end of the Chain of Craters Road (see page 64).

Kauai: The Garden Island is lush with botanical estates and Waimea Canyon, the "Grand Canyon of the Pacific" (see page 68).

The roadless Na Pali Coast on the heavenly north shore is one of the world's most challenging and majestic seaside hikes (see page 71).

Molokai: The immense, sheer seacliffs of this rugged, sparsely-populated island are the setting for the leper colony founded by Father Damien at Kalaupapa, which can be reached by mule (see page 77).

Lanai: This pineapple plantation island has become a tiny hideaway with two splendid resorts and the remains of the historic company town, Lanai City (see page 80).

for its surf; one beach town even served as the ultimate location for what was once the world's most popular TV show, *Baywatch*. Some visitors find Oahu (especially Honolulu) a paradise compromised by commercialism, but many are so taken with Oahu's beaches, galleries, gardens, and monuments, that they return year after year, never straying to a single neighboring island. Oahu, they say, has it all, whether you've come to relax or party, shop or adventure, learn or explore.

Waikiki Old & New

The surfboard – an ancient Hawaiian invention – is ubiquitous in Waikiki.

Waikiki, Honolulu's long white sand beach, is to Hawaii what Miami Beach is to Florida. Most visitors make this their first stop, and many never leave it. The beach extends 2.5 miles (4 km) from Ala Wai Canal (location of a splendid new **Honolulu Convention Center**, well worth a look), to **Diamond Head**, a picturesque extinct volcanic cone and hiking challenge. Every inch of beachfront is packed with surfers, boogie boarders, snorkelers, swimmers, strollers, and sunbathers. It is a gorgeous beach, with plenty to enjoy. The water is warm, the waves usually gentle, the sand inviting for tanning. The waves teem with surfers; boards and other wa-

Opening Hours in Oahu

Times vary and change, so check before setting out.

Battleship Missouri Memorial (Pearl Harbor, Tel. (808) 973-2494): Daily 9am–5pm. Admission fee.

Bishop Museum (1525 Bernice Street, Tel. (808) 847-3511): 9am–5pm daily. Admission fee.

Foster Botanical Gardens (50 N. Vineyard Blvd., Tel. (808) 522-7066): Daily 9am–4pm. Guided tours Monday–Friday 1pm. Admission fee.

Hanauma Bay (Kalanaianaole Highway): Wednesday–Monday 6am–7pm (to 6pm in winter). Admission fee.

Honolulu Academy of Arts (900 South Beretania Street, Tel. (808) 532-8700): Tuesday–Saturday 10am–4:30pm, Sunday 1–5pm. Closed on major national holidays. Guided tours Tuesday–Saturday 11am, Sunday 1:15pm. Admission fee. Free admission first Wednesday of month.

Iolani Palace (364 S. King St., Tel. (808) 522-0832): Tuesday–Saturday 9am–2:15pm. Royal Hawaiian Band plays at noon Friday. Admission fee. No children under 5 years.

Kawaiahao Church (957 Punchbowl St., Tel. (808) 522-1333). Sunday services 8am and 10:30 am. Free.

Kodak Hula Show (Waikiki Shell, Tel. (808) 627-3379): Tuesday–Thursday 10am–11am. Free.

Hawaii Maritime Center (Pier 7, Honolulu Harbor, Tel. (808) 536-6373): 8:30am–5pm daily. Admission fee.

Mission Houses Museum (553 S. King St., Tel. (808) 531-0481): Tuesday–Saturday 9am–4pm. Admission fee.

National Cemetery of the Pacific (Punchbowl Crater, Tel. (808) 566-1430): Daily 8am–6:30pm. Free.

Polynesian Cultural Center (Laie, Tel. (808) 293-3333): Monday–Saturday 12:30–9:30pm. Admission fee.

Queen Emma Summer Palace (2913 Pali Highway, Tel. (808) 595-3167): Daily 9am–4 pm. Admission fee.

USS Arizona Memorial (Pearl Harbor, Tel. (808) 422-0561 or 422-2771): Daily 7:30am–5:00pm. Last shuttle boat departs 3:30pm daily. Closed Thanksgiving, Christmas, New Years. Free.

"Gimme an H!" The Kodak Hula Show remains a longstanding staple of Waikiki entertainment.

tersports equipment are easily rented at kiosks; and it's one of the best places in the world to learn to surf. Outrigger canoes, ocean kayaks, catamarans, and other sightseeing vessels are also for hire. Moreover, the beach hotels (truly right on the beach) are splendid. Budget travelers can pick from an array of small hotels and condos just a block or two inland. Swimsuits are acceptable wear on and off the beach, and the sands are open to strolling and people-watching their entire length. Parallel to Waikiki are wide avenues of restaurants (from fast food to world-class dining), spacious malls, outdoor markets, art galleries, and hundreds of shops, from T-shirt kiosks and the ubiquitous ABC discount stores to Louis Vuitton. Once bordering on the shoddy and shady, Waikiki's commercial street has been upgraded; it's as pleasant to stroll as the beach itself.

Among Waikiki's leading tourist attractions are the **Waikiki Aquarium** (2777 Kalakaua Avenue), with a shark tank, a theater, a hatchery, a chambered nautilus nursery, and a reef machine that recreates a living coral reef. At the Waikiki Shell (2805 Monsarrat Avenue), just off the beach and Kalakaua Avenue, there's also the chance to watch (Tuesday–Thursday 10am; free) the **Kodak Hula Show** (now sponsored by Pleasant Hawaiian Holidays), a dance and music revue that started in 1937.

Waikiki is more than big-time surfing, shopping, and spectacle, however; it's a beach with a past, a romantic one. Among the first foreign guests to stay in Waikiki in the 19th century was the author Robert Louis Stevenson, who saw Waikiki's potential immediately. "If anyone desires such old-fashioned things as lovely scenery, quiet, pure air, clear sea water, heavenly sunsets hung out before his eyes over the Pacific and the distant hills of Waianae," he wrote, "I recommend him to Waikiki Beach."

This Old Waikiki of Hawaiian monarchs, sugar barons, taro farmers, matinee idols, surfing legends, and writers begins on Kalakaua Avenue, Waikiki's main street, named for King David Kalakaua, ruler of Hawaii from 1874 to 1891. In the late 19th century this was Waikiki Road. Downtown Honolulu was three miles away by a horse-drawn trolley. The sole accommodations for travelers consisted of the Sans Souci, a cluster of bungalows at the foot of Diamond Head built in 1884, and a few bathhouse shacks for daytime use. Most Waikiki residents were either royal Hawaiians or wealthy overseas businessmen. One of the wealthiest, Walter C. Peacock, noting an influx of tourists on arriving steamships, oversaw construction of Waikiki's first grand hotel, the four-story 75-room Moana Hotel, a beaux-arts masterpiece that opened on March 11, 1901. The first guests, a hundred Shriners, paid the stiff room rate of $1.50 per night.

From the elaborate porte cochère at the entrance to the coffered ceilings of the lobby, the Moana bespoke a European elegance. Two wings were added in 1918, when tourism had swelled to 8,000 visitors annually, and an old banyan tree became the centerpiece of the Moana's Banyan Court, for decades Hawaii's most romantic dancing and dining spot. From the Prince of Wales to Amelia Earhart, celebrities of the 1920s and 1930s gathered at the Moana. The Banyan Court is still in place. The Moana's latest renovation, completed in 1989, has restored the hotel (now the **Sheraton Moana Surfrider**) to its glory days, complete with columns, porthole windows, even

Stray Cats in Paradise

It's impossible for any pet-lover to visit Hawaii without noticing all the homeless cats that inhabit the margins of parking lots, parks, and tourist sites. Stray and feral cats are a big problem in the islands, one enhanced by the fine weather and mobile human population. But the situation isn't hopeless. At least some of the cats – a growing number – have been trapped, neutered or spayed so they don't reproduce, and then returned to their habitats and fed daily by local caretakers. On Oahu, some 1,400 people have taken responsibility for colonies of strays on Diamond Head, in downtown Honolulu near the statue of Kamehameha I, and at hundreds of other spots around the island. On Maui, guardian angels watch over 95 colonies. On Kauai, the Humane Society runs a thrift shop to support its efforts (3100 Kuhio Highway, Lihue).

Information and assistance are available at the Hawaiian Humane Society, Honolulu (Tel. (808) 946-2187; <www.hawaiianhumane.org>); the Maui Humane Society (Tel. (808) 877-3680); the Kauai Humane Society (Tel. (808) 335-5255); the Hawaii Island Humane Society headquarters in Kailua-Kona (Tel. (808) 329-1175) or satellite shelters in Waimea (Tel. (808) 885-4558) and Keaau (Tel. (808) 966-5458); Advocats in Kailua-Kona (Tel. (808) 326-3724); Animal Rescue Coalition of Hawaii in Waimea (on the Big Island, Tel. (808-987-2724); the Hawaii Cat Foundation in Honolulu (<www.hicat.org>); and Abandoned and Feral Cat Friends in Honolulu (Tel. (808) 686-CATS).

the plaster fleur-de-lis decorations, and it's worth a tour (which the hotel offers from its main desk).

The Moana Hotel's supremacy was soon challenged. Just down the beach, the Matson Steamship Company constructed an even more imposing structure, the 400-room Moorish-style Royal Hawaiian. Known to this day as the "Pink Palace," the **Royal Hawaiian Hotel** opened on 1 February 1927, and its gardens contain remnants of the "King's Grove" of royal coconut trees, which numbered 10,000 when Mark Twain visited Waikiki in 1866. (Twain likened these trees to "ladies' parasols struck by lightning.")

The pineapple was not originally Hawaiian, but arrived after Captain Cook

The Royal Hawaiian became the new celebrity favorite, attracting screen stars Douglas Fairbanks and Mary Pickford and billionaires Henry Ford II and Nelson Rockefeller. Both the Moana and the Royal Hawaiian hotels retain the early 20th-century flavor of a romantic Waikiki, where beachboys taught Hollywood stars and starlets to surf. A third hotel marks another chapter: the triumph of the high-rise. Commercial air service began to offer the first group tours to Honolulu in the 1950s, and the Matson Company's hotel division opened Waikiki's first modern high-rise tourist hotel on 11 June 1955, the **Princess Kaiulani Hotel**, at 11 stories, then Hawaii's tallest building.

Even the Princess Kaiulani Hotel resonates with echoes

Waikiki honors in bronze Hawaiian-born Olympian Duke Kahanamoku.

of older Waikiki days. It is named for the sweetest figure in the epic of Hawaiian royalty, Victoria Kaiulani, last heir to the Hawaiian throne. Born in 1875 to King David Kalakaua's sister, the young princess grew up in Waikiki on a fairy-tale estate, Ainahau, filled with peacocks, gardens, and a banyan tree planted at her christening. It was under this tree that Robert Louis Stevenson regaled the princess with stories of his adventures in the South Pacific, and where he penned a poem in the princess's guest book upon her departure for school in England in 1889.

The Princess Kaiulani Hotel is situated on the south edge of the Ainahau Estate, which has since disappeared. Victoria Kaiulani's memory is preserved in portraits on the hotel walls, including a most striking one in the lobby. In 1891, at age 16, the princess was named heir to the monarchy, but she was never to reign. In 1898, Hawaii was annexed by the United States, ending the long reign of Hawaiian kings and queens. Princess Kaiulani died the very next year at age 23 of a long illness after a spirited horse ride during a tropical rainstorm. The peacocks of the royal estate were said to have screeched in mourning on the day of her passing.

The beach itself resonates with Waikiki history, too. You'll find the bronze **Duke Kahanamoku Statue** there, honoring a Hawaiian of royal birth who captured gold medals in swimming at the 1912 and 1920 Olympics and popularized the traditional art of surfing. Steps away are the **Wizard Stones of Waikiki,** large boulders said to mark the place where four priests from Tahiti visited in the 16th century. These kahuna are believed to have imparted healing power to the stones, which vanished in the 1920s and were finally rediscovered in the 1960s under a nearby bowling alley. Nowadays so many people want to touch and rub these healing stones that a fence encircles them to ensure their preservation.

Little wonder then that King Kamehameha the Great, who unified the islands in 1810, built a home at Waikiki (where the Moana Hotel stands today). The estates and summer retreats of Kamehameha's successors and royal court continued to be situated at Waikiki, too, and even today, it's the "royal retreat" for thousands of visitors.

Honolulu

Honolulu is a busy modern American city, but with some striking differences. It is sandwiched between lush, steep green peaks and the brilliant blue Pacific shore. On one end is **Diamond Head** (so named by early sailors who thought they'd found diamonds in the crater). The crater walls and tunnels of this extinct volcanic cone make for a steep, one-mile hour-long climb, favored by hikers for the fine overlook it affords of city and ocean.

On the other side (the *ewa* side) of Honolulu is the Pearl Harbor Naval Base (see page 39), while in between is the most visited site in all of Hawaii, **Punchbowl Crater,** once the site of human sacrifices, now filled with over 30,000 graves of American veterans. Within this triangle of attractions, the big city has more major historic and cultural sites than any other location in the islands. The more of these sites you visit, the deeper your understanding of Hawaii.

The **Bishop Museum** (1525 Bernice Street) is Hawaii's premier collection of its heritage, beginning with the Polynesian voyages 1,500 years ago. There's a display of antique surfboards, including Duke Kahanamoku's original, along with royal feather cloaks, old leis, ritual statuary, and thousands of other priceless relics of old Hawaii. Established in 1889, this research complex is considered the principal museum of the Pacific. Within its venerable Hawaiian Hall of wooden staircases and carved koa wood interior trim, now under serious attack by the island's notoriously destructive termites, there are extensive displays of native artifacts, daily afternoon performances of songs and dances of the past (including the authentic hulas), and craft demonstrations performed by senior Hawaiian artisans. Among Hawaiian quilters working at the Bishop are many living legends in a craft derived from the earliest missionary days.

Near city center is a cluster of historic buildings. **Iolani Palace** (364 S. King St.) is the preeminent historic landmark in Honolulu. Built in 1882, it is the only royal palace in the United States, and served as the official residence of Hawaii's last reigning monarchs, King David Kalakaua (the "Merry Monarch") and his sister and successor, Queen Liliuokalani (who was imprisoned here for nine months when foreign businessmen overthrew the monarchy). The palace has been exquisitely restored to its full grandeur, including the throne room. The guided tours (required) specify that booties must be worn over shoes and that no pen be unsheathed or pencil used (to prevent damaging the precious interiors).

The **Queen Emma Summer Palace** (2913 Pali Highway), located on the outskirts of Honolulu, is yet another landmark in Hawaii's royal past. This small mansion was built in 1843

Iolani Palace in downtown Honolulu is the only royal palace in the United States.

as the home of King Kamehameha IV and his wife, Queen Emma. It is filled with personal heirlooms and period furnishings. The décor is more Victorian than Hawaiian, since its royal Hawaiian residents were as much at home with European and American ways as with their own rapidly disappearing Pacific island traditions.

Back downtown, within sight of Iolani Palace, is the **Mission Houses Museum** (553 S. King St.), a living history exhibit that illustrates a crucial chapter in Hawaii's heritage. The three buildings which housed the first American Protestant missionaries were built between 1820 and 1841. The daily life of the missionaries is recreated within the oldest frame house in Hawaii (shipped from Boston in 1821) and the old coral-block print shop with its replica of the first printing press, still used for demonstrations. Across the street from the Mission Houses

Museum is **Kawaiahao Church** (957 Punchbowl St.), dedicated in 1842, making it one of Hawaii's oldest places of Christian worship. The 1,000-pound coral blocks that make up its walls were cut from Oahu's ocean reefs. Visitors can attend Sunday services here, some of which are conducted in Hawaiian. This is also the location of the missionary cemetery, consecrated in 1823, burial site of the first proselytizers and some of their children, who later established Hawaii's sugar and plantation dynasties. The striking shrine next to the church is the **King Lunalilo Mausoleum**, final resting place of Hawaii's first elected monarch, who followed Kamehameha V to the throne in 1872.

At the **Hawaii Maritime Center** (Pier 7, Honolulu Harbor), the varied strands of Honolulu's seafaring tradition, from outrigger canoes and whaling ships to ancient surfboards and Pan Am airplanes, are drawn together. The world's last remaining four-masted full-rigged ship (Falls of Clyde), dating from 1878, is moored beside the museum.

Just down the harbor is the recently remodeled **Aloha Tower Marketplace**, with its shops and food court. Once the depot for arriving steamships and ocean liners, it now welcomes modern cruise ships that offer nostalgic weekly sailings to the neighboring islands. The days of Grand Tours and steamer trunks are also evoked at the swank **Louis Vuitton** outlet (2200 Kalakaua Avenue) in the heart of Waikiki on the former site of Gump's of San Francisco.

At the back of the store in large glass cases there's an assortment of the historic made-to-order rigid luggage that Louis Vuitton began offering to travelers in 1854. Among the zinc trunks and striped canvas bags dating from the late 19th and early 20th centuries are a monogrammed linen trunk, manufactured in 1919, that transforms into a writing desk, a wardrobe in monogrammed canvas from 1938 that belonged to American cowboy actor Rory Calhoun, a toilet set created in cowhide, ebony, and silver for the musician Paderewski, and a reproduction of the Red Cross case used in World War I.

Honolulu's Asian influence is most pronounced in its **Chinatown**, a marvelous cultural quarter to stroll, with its dim sum and noodle factories, Asian markets and cafés, Kuan Yin Temple (the oldest Chinese temple in Hawaii), and a burgeoning new collection of art galleries and shops featuring native crafts, topped off by the newly-restored 1,400-seat beaux-arts **Hawaii Theater** (1130 Bethel Street). Several streets in Chinatown (especially Maunakea Street) are lined with lei shops, where selection and price are excellent.

The **Honolulu Academy of Arts** (900 South Beretania Street) is a pleasant surprise for many gallery-goers. Not only does this 1927 academy with its landscaped courtyards house a fine Oriental collection, but it is also home to major works from America and Europe.

Nor is Honolulu devoid of showplaces for Hawaii's extraordinary flora and fauna. The oldest botanical preserve in the state, the **Foster Botanic Gardens** (50 North Vineyard Boulevard) consists of 13.5 acres (5.5 hectares) with over 5,000 species, headlined by its orchid collection.

Pearl Harbor

When Japan launched its surprise attack on the US fleet in Honolulu's **Pearl Harbor**, 7 December 1941, the battleship Arizona was among many of the vessels sunk. It remains just where it went down that day, a tomb for the 1,777 men aboard. The **USS Arizona Memorial**, a white archway built over the sunken vessel, became a national shrine in 1962. The National Park Service conducts daily tours via launches that depart from the Visitors' Center on shore, preceded by a moving documentary film employing actual footage of the attack. The film,

Inside the USS Arizona Memorial, honoring those who perished in the attack on Pearl Harbor.

boat ride, and browsing time on the memorial (from where you can see the upper deck of the Arizona in the shallow waters, its turrets above the waves, the hull still slowly leaking oil) take about 75 minutes.

Next door to the USS Arizona Memorial Visitors' Center is the site of the **USS Bowfin Submarine Museum & Park**, where you can roam an actual World War II submarine during a self-guided tour. The submarine, anchored in Pearl Harbor, is impressive; so, too, are the plaques ashore that record the fascinating, heroic stories of the US submarine fleet and the 3,500 submariners who never returned from the sea.

The newest attraction at Pearl Harbor is the **Battleship Missouri Memorial**. It's worth booking the guided tour for a full exploration of this commanding vessel where World War II ended, docked within sight of the USS Arizona Memorial (and served by shuttle buses from the Bowfin parking lot). It was on board the *Missouri* that General MacArthur accepted the surrender of the Japanese military on September 2, 1945.

Beyond Honolulu

The leeward (westward), windward (eastward), and north coasts of Oahu are each worth exploring by car. The west side of the island is the least crowded. Its major new attraction is **Ko Olina** (on Aliinui Drive, Kapolei), a development that includes a luxury hotel (JW Marriott Ihilani Resort), golf course, condos, and along its beaches, a series of beautiful lagoons that are open to the public for picnicking, water activities, and hiking. The beach stroll here is a pleasure; a paved walkway undulates along the rough and rugged coastline. Farther north up the west coast, where the folded cliffs steepen dramatically, there is the ancient **Kaneaki Heiau**, a 15th century Hawaiian temple to the god Lono, provider of fertile crops. The entrance is through the Makaha Resort; ask for directions and hours at the resort gate. **Makaha Beach Park** is for championship surfing; in fact, this is where modern professional surfing originated in Hawaii.

The towns on the west shore are not tourist traps, nor are they upscale suburbs, but part of the "real" Hawaii, with substantial native Hawaiian and Pacific islander populations. (Some of the residents are said to be abrupt with outsiders treading on their home ground.) The highway ends at Keawaula Bay, a surfing beach with big winter waves. There's no road connecting the west and north shores.

To reach the north coast, you'll need to drive up the east shore or across central Oahu. The east route (Kalanianaole Highway out of Honolulu) has a number of superb attractions, led by **Hanauma Bay** (east of Diamond Head). The most famous snorkeling spot on Oahu, Hanauma is an old volcanic cone missing its seaward wall. The ocean has filled in the shallow crater floor, creating a protected crescent-shaped bay of lava, coral, and schools of reef fish. Its sheer beauty has attracted Hollywood (*Blue Hawaii* with Elvis, *From Here to Eternity* with Burt Lancaster and Deborah Kerr), along with great hordes of snorkelers, so be sure to arrive as early as possible (just after sunrise) to get a parking spot and elbow room. It's a long walk down the crater side to the beach, but a shuttle is available. You can rent snorkeling gear in Honolulu or in the crater, where fast food is also sold. Hanauma Bay is currently closed Tuesdays, but you should check on the schedule before setting out.

Beyond Hanauma Bay are some of Oahu's prettiest beaches, including **Sandy Beach** and **Makapuu Beach**, both rather treacherous for swimming, but renowned for bodysurfing. From Makapuu Beach, there's a great view of Sharkfin and Rabbit islands. **Sea Life Park** (41-202 Kalanianaole Highway, Tel. (808) 259-7933), which contains the **Pacific Whaling Museum**'s enormous scrimshaw and artifact collections, is one of Hawaii's most popular family stops. The park is noted for its dolphin shows and hands-on educational marine exhibits.

Kailua is the best known of Honolulu's bedroom communities on the windward side, but it is better appreciated by active locals for its wide beaches (including Lanikai Beach) where swimming and bodysurfing are safe and windsurfing has a field day. For an overview of the windward side and its long valleys, follow the signs up to **Nuuanu Pali Lookout** (off the Pali Highway), a windy 1,000-ft (305-m) high ledge where King Kamehameha the Great's forces ran the enemy armies off the cliffsides in 1795.

The main coastal route, the Kahekili Highway, continues north, but take a detour to the **Byodo-In Temple** (47-200 Kahekili Highway). This temple, opened in 1968, is a copy of an ancient Buddhist temple in Japan. Set against some of Oahu's most towering green cliffs, this shrine may very well take your breath away. There's a bronze bell to strike, peacocks strutting outside the prayer hall, and a carp pond where birds eat out of your hand. Another stunning landscape just after the

The Nuuanu Pali Lookout offers views of the cliff and valley where Kamehameha the Great fought in 1795.

temple is **Senator Fong's Plantation and Gardens** (47-285 Pulama Road, Tel. (808) 239-6775). This is the 725-acre (294-hectare) botanical estate of Hawaii's former senator. Guided tram tours give you close-up views of dozens of varieties of flowers, trees, and tropical fruits.

Ahead are two more major attractions, established by the Mormon community (Church of Jesus Christ of Latter-day Saints), who maintain a branch of Utah's Brigham Young University (BYU) nearby. The **Mormon Temple** in the tiny town of Laie opened in 1919; Mormon missionaries came to this community in 1864. The **Polynesian Cultural Center** (55-370 Kamehameha Highway, Laie) takes an entertaining theme-park approach to demonstrating the culture and traditions of Polynesia and Hawaii, with BYU students stringing leis and pounding poi, canoe processions on the streams, and hula performances on stage. A tour of the grounds can take a full day, capped by an optional evening luau.

The drive up the east side to the North Shore weaves through taro patches, orchid farms, and cattle ranches pressed between the foothills of the Koolau Mountain peaks and the beaches with the big waves. At Kualoa Beach Park there's an islet called **Chinaman's Hat**, a sacred place of refuge and the retreat of Hawaiian royalty in the old days. Just beyond, at Kahuku, there's the picturesque **Kuoloa Sugar Mill**, built in 1873 and shut down in 1971. Its doors are still open; you can take a free glance at the massive original equipment inside, then shop the fabric stalls nearby for bargains on sarongs. Keep an eye out for vendor trucks parked along the road selling the celebrated local shrimp and other fresh seafood; these treats are inexpensive, tasty, and favored by locals.

Sugar plantations once dominated Oahu's North Shore; now, surfing is king. **Sunset Beach**, the "Banzai Pipeline" at **Ehukai Beach**, sandy **Waimea Beach**, and **Haleiwa Beach** are among the most famous in world surfdom. The high waves that bring the world's best surfers here for winter competition are too much for swimmers, but you can entertain yourself by watching the surfers or surveying the surf shops, galleries, and shave ice stands in towns like Haleiwa or Waialua.

If you return to Honolulu on the high road (Kamehameha Highway) across the central plateau of sugarcane and pineapple fields, take a break at the **Dole Plantation** (64-1550 Kamehameha Highway, Route 99). Surrounded by red soil fields and oceans of green pineapple, the visitor's center offers a gift shop, demonstration gardens, and what the Guinness Book of World Records assures us is the world's biggest maze.

MAUI

The island of Maui has become Oahu's chief rival for tourism. Many visitors prefer Maui: It is less populated and offers more outdoor scenery and activities, with more swimmable beaches than any other island. A growing number of direct flights connect Maui to the US mainland, and American Hawaii Cruises has given its *SS Independence* cruise ship a new home port at

The Greening of Maui

From wide sandy beaches to dense rain forests, from fresh lava flows to the alpine tundra of a volcanic rim in the clouds, Maui is a natural treasure-house, where life evolved slowly, a new plant or creature appearing just once every 10,000 years. Today over 100,000 wilderness acres, from the summit of Haleakala volcano to the Keanae coast, are under the protection of the East Maui Watershed Partnership, preserving the highest concentration of rare and endangered birds in the world. Along the shores, the Maui Land & Pineapple Company has turned two of Kapalua's six crescent bays into marine preserves so that swimmers, snorkelers and divers can enjoy the coral, reef fish, manta rays, and green sea turtles there. Molokini, the extinct volcano just off the Wailea shore and one of the biggest snorkeling attractions in Hawaii, has also become a marine preserve. In fact, the waters surrounding Maui are part of a federal marine sanctuary established by the US Congress in 1992. Humpback whales are the most notable beneficiary of the greening of Maui's ocean waters, but visitors are beneficiaries, too, since the whales are now so plentiful here that one often sees them from shore December through April. The Pacific Whale Foundation, Maui's oldest marine conservation organization, offers workshops year-round on whales, dolphins, and coral, as well as whale-watching, snorkeling, and sunset barbecue cruises.

Other "green activities" for Maui visitors include "Star Grazing on the Green" at Kapalua's Plantation Golf Course, an environmental program run by the Hawaii Nature Center and the Kapalua Nature Society; guided hikes into the east Maui wilderness preserve, conducted by the Nature Conservancy and the Park Service; and horseback riding on the slopes of the Haleakala volcano, arranged through hotels, ranches, and private stables.

Kahului, Maui, from which it now departs on a four-island seven-night voyage every Sunday (after a day of Maui tours). If the Hawaiian Islands are a travel paradise, then Maui ranks as the paradise of paradises; year after year, America's top travel magazines have rated Maui as the "best island in the world." Perhaps what makes Maui so attractive is its diversity – from perfect beaches to sweeping golf courses, from lava peaks to rain forests, from glitzy malls to world-class resorts.

Maui consists of two distinct land masses, both dominated by huge volcanoes. West Maui has lush tropical gardens, legendary beach resorts built on wide lava flows, and the old whaling town of Lahaina. East Maui is even more diverse, with big resorts, black sand beaches, top snorkeling and diving sites, the Mount Haleakala crater, and the challenging road to Hana, which twists through a prehistoric landscape.

The big resorts are distributed in clusters along the west coast of Maui, running from Kapalua and Kaanapali south to Wailea and Makena. Activities include windsurfing, parasailing, driving the Hana Highway (54 bridges in 54 winding miles), glass-bottom boat trips and snorkel sails to Molokini (a submerged volcanic crater just offshore), helicopter rides, charter fishing, charter sailing, gallery and boutique shopping, swimming, surfing, golfing, tennis, and horseback riding – just about everything. The four most important areas to explore are Lahaina town (with its whaling history and shopping), Iao Valley State Park (with its lush tropical forests), Haleakala National Park (with the world's largest dormant volcano), and Hana (with its remote road into pretty Hawaiian scenery and old traditions).

Lahaina & West Maui

 The whaling port of **Lahaina** is at the heart of West Maui, at the foot of the West Maui Mountains. Now a National Historic Landmark, Lahaina was the royal capital of old Hawaii when

The Carthaginian II, a floating museum, recalls the turbulent whaling days of Lahaina.

the whaling ships began arriving in 1819. Among the seamen who called on this raw and rollicking town was Herman Melville, who would one day write his own epics about whales and remote Pacific Islands.

Lahaina today has capitalized on its romantic past by becoming a quaint shopping town and something of a tourist trap (selling more scrimshaw jewelry than any other city in the world). Along crowded Front Street are dozens of boutiques, over 40 galleries, and some fine seafood restaurants, but you'll also find a collection of well-maintained historic public buildings, such as the **Masters and Mates Reading Room**, the **Seamen's Hospital**, the **Wo Hing Society House** (built 1912, Hawaii's oldest surviving Chinese community Tong house), and the **Baldwin House**, a restored 1830s missionary home, now a museum. A single monumental banyan tree enfolds the spa-

Wailuku, the former stomping grounds of Mark Twain, retains the distinctive look of Old Maui.

cious town square, where the courthouse still stands. In one corner of the square there's a reconstructed remnant of the **Lahaina Fort**, built in 1831 to introduce law and order to the sailors' town (it was torn down in 1854). The harbor, once home to 400 whaling ships at a time, is graced by a replica of the old lighthouse and a restored two-masted sailing brig, the **Carthaginian II**, which serves as a whaling museum.

Off Front Street to the north is an arresting and unexpected shrine, the **Jodo Mission** (12 Ala Moana Street), built to commemorate the centennial of the first Japanese immigration to Hawaii. There's a sandy graveyard to one side and the largest Amida Buddha statue outside of Japan in the temple courtyard.

The northern end of West Maui has some luxury resorts, as well as reasonably-priced condos and family-style hotels at Napili and Kahana, where the island of Molokai rises across the channel and the sunsets are gorgeous. Inland, West Maui is dominated by the sculpted volcanic peaks and dramatic valleys, some of which have been barely explored.

Wailuku, the market town of wooden storefronts where Mark Twain once lived, is the gateway to **Iao Valley State Park**, where a stone pillar, the 2,250-ft (686-m) high **Iao Needle**, presides over the spectacular terrain (Twain dubbed it the "Yosemite of the Pacific"), a natural garden crisscrossed with hiking paths. Here King Kamehameha the Great completed his conquest of Maui in a 1790 battle. Scores of royal Hawaiians were buried in the surrounding caves. On the road from Wailuku to the Iao Valley, the Hawaii Nature Center's recently renovated **Iao Valley Interactive Science Arcade** offers a fine overview of Maui's ecology through its many hands-on exhibits, touch pools, aquariums and a glass solarium that overlooks the valley's rain forest. On the same valley road are the **Kepaniwai Park and Heritage Gardens**, with pavilions and landscape gardens devoted to Hawaii's ethnic traditions, from native Hawaiian to Japanese and Chinese designs.

Back at Wailuku, there's the 1833-built **Bailey House**, a missionary school and residence that became a museum in 1885, where you can see a large collection of early artifacts including outrigger canoes, redwood surfboards, and quilts. A plantation town, Wailuku has a formidable 1907 courthouse and the 1928 art deco **Iao Theater**. Adventurous drivers can take the treacherous pass road (Highway 340) that skirts the northeast coast of West Maui (a route rental cars usually aren't allowed to travel).

Highway 30, running south from Wailuku, marks the inland dividing line between West Maui and East Maui. Here you'll find large fields of pineapple and sugarcane. The 112-acre (45-hectare) **Maui Tropical Plantation and Country Store** has guided tram tours through Maui's plantation history.

Maui's Southwest Coast

The western shores of East Maui were hardly touched by resort development until the 1970s. The coastal road still reaches a dead end south of **Makena** and a golden stretch of sands favored by locals, who call it Oneola Beach or just the Big Beach. The southwest tip of Maui has some fine little snorkeling spots, a black sand beach, and Maui's most recent lava flow (about 1790). Makena is also the location of a splendid seaside shrine, the **Keawaiai Church**, built in 1855, with picturesque headstones in its cemetery.

There are fine beaches all the way along the southwest shoreline. The longest white-sand beach is **Wailea**. Wailea is the location of some of the world's most fabulous luxury resorts (Grand Wailea, Four Seasons, Kea Lani, Renaissance, Outrigger). They face Maui's top offshore snorkeling destination, **Molokini**, an islet that is actually a submerged volcanic cone. A crescent of the crater wall rises from the sea, and dozens of excursion boats anchor near it. Molokini is reason enough to join a snorkel or sight-seeing cruise. The marine life within this sea cone is stunning.

Water tours to Molokini depart daily, usually from Maalaea Harbor, where East and West Maui meet. Maalaea is also the location of the new **Maui Ocean Center**, North America's largest tropical aquarium. South of here the road runs through the **Kealia Pond National Wildlife Refuge**, where you should keep an eye out for endangered green sea turtles. Turtles are frequent companions at many spots along the west side of East Maui, particularly at **Kihei**. Kihei is also the location of the **Hawaiian Islands Humpback Whale National Marine Sanctuary**, near the ancient fish pond of Koieie. Humpback whales calve and nurse their young in Maui's waters after spending their summers 3,500 miles (2,170 km) north in

Alaska. Whales put on their breech-and-spout shows from December to April in Hawaii. For whale-watching from Maui's shores, which seem blessed with more than their share of leviathan pods, February and March are the prime months.

Upcountry to Mount Haleakala

Mount Haleakala, the largest dormant volcano on Earth, dominates East Maui. Its western slopes, referred to as the Upcountry, are cooler, afford fine panoramic views, and contain Maui onion fields, fruit and flower farms, cattle ranches, and even a winery. These sleepy slopes with views, flowers, and gentle temperatures have become popular places to live, too. On your way to or from the volcano, don't overlook the pleasures of a drive along the western slopes. You can begin the journey Upcountry with a tour of the **Alexander and Baldwin Sugar Museum**, located in the superintendent's 1902 plantation house,

Enjoy the vast views from the summit of Mount Haleakala, the largest dormant volcano on Earth.

next door to a century-old working cane mill, surrounded by historic plantation equipment; then take a small rural road through cactus-infested land that will remind you of the Baja Peninsula to the town of Kula (elevation 3,200 ft/975 m).

The white eight-sided jewel of a church at Kula, known as the **Holy Ghost Catholic Church** (built 1894–1897), was a gift from the King and Queen of Portugal to the Portuguese plantation workers of Maui who arrived in the late 1870s. South along the Kula Highway are two places to quench your thirst. **Grandma's Maui Coffee** uses a century-old roaster, local beans, and a grandmother's recipe for its brews. Then, past a Chinese park and cemetery dedicated to Sun Yat-sen near Keokea (Maui's tiny Chinatown), comes the tasting room of **Tedeschi Vineyards** (elevation 2,000 ft/610 m), Hawaii's first and most upscale winery. Its sparkling wines have been served in the White House. The vineyard property is encompassed by the historic Ulupalakua cattle ranch, the site of VIP gatherings in the days of Hawaii's monarchy.

The peak of the Upcountry experience is **Haleakala National Park**, topped by a lunar caldera 21 miles (34 km) around and 3,000 ft (915 m) deep. (Lunar is not an idle adjective here; US astronauts trained on Mount Haleakala for the moon landing.) As the 10,023-ft (3,055-m) summit of this great volcano is often in the clouds, many visitors who set out before dawn to view the Maui sunrise are disappointed when the relentless fog prevents a view – even of the crater. The crater and the vistas sometimes clear out later in the day, and the switchback drive (which takes about 90 minutes from downtown Kahului) is more impressive in daylight.

On top there's a Visitors' Center, a research complex (Science City), hiking trails, crater overlooks, and a field of rare silversword. Mystics have dubbed this the strongest natural power point in America. It's certainly one of the most scenic on a clear day (when many of the other islands are visible), and it's also apt to be 30 degrees cooler than at sea level. The great sport on Haleakala is to coast down to the sea on specially-designed bicycles, a feat that the bicycle tour companies claim nearly anyone can safely manage. The ride back from the volcano isn't all downhill. There are plenty of high points, such as a stop at **Makawao**, a Wild West town where *paniolos* (Hawaiian cowboys) still work the ranches and the townsfolk maintain some of Hawaii's best art galleries.

Hana

The last unspoiled frontier of Hawaiian tourism is traversed on the remarkable road to **Hana**. Hana is located on the eastern tip of Maui, where waterfalls, taro patches, sacred native sites, and the lushest of tropical gardens are creased into the remote coastal landscape. The road from Kahului to Hana measures just 54 miles (87 km), but it is a slow, dangerous drive with over 600 hairpin turns and more than 50 one-lane bridges where right-of-way is sometimes indicated, sometimes not. Take your time; start with a full tank of gas, pack a lunch, and set out very early. You can buy provisions at the hip, bustling little burg of **Paia**, a few miles east along the Hana Highway (while it's still straight). Return late, if possible, since by mid-morning or mid-afternoon, traffic slows to a crawl.

Driving the Hana Highway is a consuming experience, but it's worth pulling off to see something of the remarkable terrain. There are waterfalls and natural rock-lined swimming pools at **Twin Falls** (mile marker 2) and **Puohokamoa Falls** (mile marker 11), both requiring hikes into the jungle. To see where the opening sequence of Jurassic Park was filmed, visit the **Garden of Eden Arboretum and Botanical Garden** (mile marker 10), a showcase of Hawaii's native plants. At mile marker 17, you can take a side road down to the Hawaiian village of

Keanae, past an 1860 church and taro fields, to a rough and primitive black lava beach. The **Keanae Arboretum**, always open, is bursting with native and tropical plants and trees; its streamside pools are made for wading and swimming.

The town of Hana is a small coastal village of big banyans, bamboo, and plumeria. It's home to a magnificent cottage complex, the **Hotel Hana-Maui**, which dates back to 1946; today, the hotel is an expensive, very private, completely relaxing beach resort. The **Hana Museum Cultural Center** (4974 Uakea Road) is sometimes open, sometimes not; the courthouse next door dates from 1871 and the large **Wananalua Congregational Church** from 1842. The picturesque, crammed-to-the-rafters **Hasegawa General Store** carries almost everything.

The **Red Sand Beach** (Kaihalulu Beach), approachable only via a highly treacherous trail along a cinder cone near the big hotel, is a protected snorkeling beach of very red granules set like rubies in the remnants of a scoured-out cinder cone. It will quite literally take your breath away. The **Piilanihale Heiau**, north of the Hana Airport, is another spellbinder. It's Hawaii's largest ancient outdoor temple and quite well-preserved, remaining overgrown until the 1970s and secret for centuries.

> Visitors who carry home lava rocks or black beach sand are inviting misfortune, according to many local people.

Rather than fight the traffic back the way you came, it is now easier to complete the circle and continue past Hana all the way back to Ulupalakua and the Tedeschi Vineyards on the west side of the island. The distance isn't much more, the road is straighter, the unpaved sections now only account for a few miles, and there are things to see along the way. First is **Hamoa Beach**, Hana's best swimming and snorkeling beach. About a 30-minute up-

and-down drive beyond Hana is the inaccurately named **Seven Sacred Pools**, more properly called **Oheo Gulch**. The pools (actually several dozen of them) and the waterfalls that interlace them are stacked terrace upon terrace on a steep jungle cliff that rises from the seashore (the "high-rise hot tubs of paradise," one local termed them). The **Kipahulu Ranger Station** has information about hiking and camping options here, where 0.5- and 1.5-mile (0.8-/2.8-km) trails to the pools begin in the parking lot.

Sacred Pools – Oheo Gulch attracts visitors with its otherworldly waterfalls.

Beyond the sacred pools, past the old St. Paul's Catholic Church and the ruins of a sugar mill, is the seaside **Palapala Hoomau Congregational Church**, built in 1857. It's a plain little church that attracts many visitors, most to pay homage at **Lindbergh's Grave**. Aviator Charles A. Lindbergh (1902–1974) lived his last years in the exquisite seclusion of Hana.

This "other road from Hana" continues around the island as the Piilani Highway Route 31. While the road can be rough and subject to seasonal closures due to washouts, it can also be a much faster, less crowded, far straighter way back to civilization. The jungles of Hana disappear, as do the tedious twists and turns, and desolate fields of lava from Mount Haleakala dominate the uninhabited seascape.

HAWAII – THE BIG ISLAND

The Big Island of Hawaii is the Texas of the islands: the biggest (more land than all the other islands combined), the most southern, the youngest (a mere million years old), and the most volcanically active. The Big Island is relatively vast, with a varied terrain (from rain forests to deserts, from beaches to snow-capped peaks, interlaced with recent lava flows). It receives far fewer visitors than Oahu or Maui, but attracts adventurers, romantics, and those who want to escape even farther from civilization.

The birthplace of King Kamehameha the Great, unifier of the Hawaiian islands, and home to the goddess Pele, Hawaii's fiery creator, the Big Island is the foremost island of volcanoes. Mauna Kea is the tallest from sea level (13,796 ft/4,206 m), Mauna Loa the tallest from the seabed (30,000 ft/9,150 m), but the Kilauea volcano is the most active, the flashy showpiece of Hawaii Volcanoes National Park – the Big Island's number one attraction. The Big Island is loaded with other attractions, too, including Hilo, one of the lushest areas in Hawaii; Waimea, where Hawaiian cowboys still work the huge Parker Ranch; the Kohala Coast, where Hawaii's very best resorts are hidden; and the Kona Coast, celebrated for sunny beaches, ancient temples, and rich coffee.

Kohala Coast

The west coast of the Big Island, running north from the main Keahole-Kona International Airport, looks positively lunar, with little black fields of lava on every side down to the blue shores. Nearly all that breaks the haunting desolation of cooled magma are white coral stones that passersby have grouped on the black canvas to spell out messages, mostly declarations of love. About 4 miles (6.4 km) north of the airport, on the seaward side of

The beach at Waikoloa on the Big Island is a favorite of snorkelers and green sea turtles.

the Queen Kaahumanu Highway, is **Kona Coast State Park** (closed Wednesdays). Blessed with a beach of coral sands running like a ribbon between the lava and the sea, the 1.5-mile (2.4-km) road to this beach is one of the bumpiest ever built. What's most startling is the appearance in the heart of this no-man's lava land of some of the most exquisite beach resorts and golf courses on the planet.

There's the **Kona Village Resort**, once reachable only by helicopter; the **Four Seasons Hualalai**, with its 19th century-style bungalows and golf course designed by Jack Nicklaus; the **Hilton Waikoloa Village**, a fantasy resort of canal boats and a swim-with-the-dolphins pool; the newly-remodeled **Outrigger Waikoloa Beach**, with its ancient lagoon; the stately **Mauna Lani Bay Hotel and Bungalows**, with its prehistoric fish ponds and turtle preserve; the elegant **Orchid at Mauna Lani**, with a thousand works of art; the **Hapuna Beach Hotel**, on one of the island's very best beaches; and the legendary **Mauna Kea Beach Hotel**, the dream project of Laurance Rockefeller, which set the high Kohala Coast standard when it opened in 1965. These grand resorts with scores of tall palm trees and richly green gardens and golf links seem to have erupted from the lava like magical desert springs.

The **Kohala Coast** resorts, north of Kona, are attractions in themselves. The Mauna Kea Beach Hotel is worth touring just to see its Oriental art collection, headlined by the 7th-century Indian statue of Buddha in the hotel gardens. The Mauna Kea's beach (open to the public) is also extraordinary. The best beaches of all are those south of the Mauna Lani Hotel's fish and turtle ponds (where the green sea turtles sometimes even come on shore) and at the northern end of Hapuna Beach State Park, where bodysurfing gives way to snorkeling. The Orchid at Mauna Lani also maintains the **Puako Petroglyph Archaeological Park**, site of some of the island's most impressive ancient Hawaiian stone carvings.

The **Puukohola Heiau National Historic Site** (south of the fishing village of Kawaihae) contains one of the largest and best-preserved Hawaiian temples (heiau) on the islands. The lava rocks and stones of its surviving walls have stood in place without mortar since 1790, when King Kamehameha the Great built it to honor his god of war. Within the grounds is **Spencer Beach Park**, safe for swimming, fine for snorkeling, and open for camping. Beyond this ancient site of human sacrifices, the road rises into deep forests, leaving the barren expanses of black lava behind.

The more northerly reaches of the Kohala Coast are filled with towns that time seems to have forgotten, that the large rainforests seem to be bent upon reclaiming. In the town of Kapaau, fronting the courthouse, there's a remarkable **Statue of King Kamehameha the Great**. It resembles the more renowned one stationed near Iolani Palace in Honolulu, but this statue is the original. The Hawaiian government commissioned the statue in 1878 to mark the centennial of Captain Cook's arrival. Sculpted in Florence, Italy, and cast in bronze in Paris, it sank with the ship rounding Cape Horn. Another statue was cast, reaching Honolulu in time for the Merry Monarch's (David Kalakaua) coronation in 1883. Then the original turned up, salvaged and a bit worse for wear. It finally ended up in this little town where the first great monarch was born.

The coast highway (Route 270) ends at the **Pololu Valley Lookout**, where there's a grand view of wild seacliffs rising from a valley of taro farms. A short but steep trail leads down to a black sand beach.

Waimea & Mauna Kea

Hawaii's cowboy country is epitomized by the cool upland ranch lands between Kona and Hilo in the north central plateau of the Big Island. Cowboys first came to the **Waimea** area at the request of King Kamehameha II in the 1830s from Spain and Mexico. Today's *paniolos* riding the range come from the pastiche of Hawaii's Japanese, Chinese, Filipino, and Portuguese immigrant population. The centerpiece of this Wild West tradition is the **Parker Ranch**, founded by John Parker, who jumped ship in 1809, corralled some of King Kamehameha the Great's wild steers, and married the King's granddaughter. Visitors can roam the 225,000-acre (91,125-hectare) ranch and tour the original homestead at the **Parker Ranch Visitor Center and Museum** (open daily; admission fee; Tel. (808) 885-7655). The **Waimea General Store** on nearby Parker Square has some great tourist-oriented shopping.

The other great attraction in the north-central mass of the Big Island is towering **Mauna Kea**, the tallest mountain in the world when measured from the sea floor. Its summit is high

Follow me to the summit of Mauna Kea, the tallest mountain in the world when measured from its base at the sea floor.

enough from sea level (13,796 ft/4,206 m) to attract skiers in the depths of winter (but there are no lifts) and the air is among the purest on earth. Cars are permitted to drive up the slopes as high as the **Onizuka Visitor Center** at an elevation of 9,600 ft (2,926 m) (Tel. (808) 961-2180; closed Wednesdays). It was named for Hawaii's first astronaut (victim of the ill-fated Challenger explosion), and there are trails, displays, and evening telescope viewings starting at 6:30pm, Thursday–Sunday.

Mauna Kea's summit contains the world's largest concentration of observatories, staffed by 11 nations. Most of the northern and southern skies are visible from here. Only four-wheel vehicles are allowed to traverse the road from the visitor center to the top, but guided tours can be arranged (Tel. (808) 775-7121) on Tuesdays, Thursdays, and Saturdays. The summit has its own educational center, viewpoints, trails, and the world's largest telescope. The cluster of astronomical domes is stunning, as is the alpine terrain, but the air is thin, and the high elevation afflicts many a visitor with headaches, dizziness, shortness of breath, and other symptoms of altitude sickness – all of which may be worth the view from Hawaii's highest point.

Kona

The Kona coast on the southwest side of the Big Island is a sunny beach-roamers' paradise. **Kailua-Kona** is the main shopping town. Along its harbor is the lava and coral **Hulihee Palace** (75-5718 Alii Drive). Built in 1838 as a summer retreat of Hawaii's royals, it's now a museum featuring Queen Kapiolani's four-poster bed. Across the street is the oldest church on the island, the 1836 **Mokuaikaua Church** with its 112-ft (34-m) steeple. Stroll the promenade down to the Kailua Pier, where fishing, parasailing, submarine rides, and outrigger canoeing are offered. This cove is home to the picture-perfect **Ahuena Heiau**, from which Kamehameha the Great ruled all of Hawaii and where he died in 1819. Dedicated to the god of fertility, Lono, the restored temple and oracle tower facing the sea are dazzling royal monuments.

South of Kailua-Kona, near the town of Keauhou, there's a pretty Catholic shrine, the **Little Blue Church**, built in 1889, and what is now one of the shore's best spots to snorkel with the turtles, **Kahaluu Beach Park**. The coconut groves next door (on the grounds of the Ohana Keauhou Beach Resort) were favored by Hawaii's kings, as was the bathing pool. Farther down the coast is **Captain Cook's Monument**, facing the bay where he met his end in 1779. The pillar requires a difficult hike down to the beach; it is most easily viewed from the dive boats that tie up here because of the outstanding snorkeling reefs. Just beyond here is the **St. Benedict's Painted Church**, decorated inside with scenes from the Bible painted around 1900 at the behest of Father Damien, the Belgian priest who founded the leper colony at Molokai (see page 77).

The southern Kona Coast is the location of one of the largest, most impressive sacred sites of ancient Hawaii, **Puuhonua O Honaunau (City of Refuge)**, a national historic park. Honaunau Bay is open 7:30am–8pm daily; there is an admission fee (Tel. (808) 328-2326). This was truly a holy sanctuary in ancient times, where those who had broken the laws of the kapu system escaped to seek protection and absolution from the priests. A great wall of lava rock encircles two temples (heiau); the Kaahumanu Stone by the wall was where the King's wife once took refuge herself. The lava peninsula juts into the sea; the grounds are dotted with huts, coconut groves, fish ponds, idols, petroglyphs, and a visitors' center.

The hills above the Kona Coast are creased with macadamia nut groves and coffee plantations. The **Kona Coast Macadamia Nut & Candy Factory** (just off Middle Keei Road) is a good place to pick up fresh snacks and "seconds"

from the farm. World-renowned Kona coffee can be sampled at many plantation outlets in the hills. **Kona Blue Sky Coffee** (Route 182, south of Holualoa) offers walking tours Monday–Saturday 9am–3:30pm. **Greenwell Farms** has daily coffee tours, too (except on Sundays); it's next door to the **Kona Historical Society Museum** (Monday–Friday 9am–3pm).

Tiki gods still reign at Puuhonua O Honaunau City of Refuge.

The **Royal Kona Coffee Mill & Museum** on Middle Keei Road has a free tour of the old mill daily, with all the coffee you're up to sampling.

South Point

The Kona Coast gives way to the **Kau District**, the most southern region in the US. You'll pass through it if you drive this way on the Mamalahoa Highway (Route 11) to Hawaii Volcanoes National Park. There are two unforgettable sites along the way. The first is **Ka Lae (South Point)**, 11 miles (18 km) off the highway on a semi-paved one-lane road of windswept grasses. Past a wind farm of 37 high-tech, weather-beaten wind turbines in a cow field, beyond an eerie satellite dish called the "Universal Space Network," this road ends mercifully at a drop-off of sheer black cliffs – the southernmost point of land in the US. A few local fishermen ply the remote bay, where it is said the very first Polynesians reached Hawaii over 1,500 years ago. Two miles east is the South Point Information Center and parking lot for the hike to Green Sands Beach, a remote swimming hole indeed.

Mark Twain rode down this way on horseback, planting a monkeypod tree that still stands in the village of **Waiohinu**. Twain noted that "trees and flowers flourish luxuriantly" in the region. The next town on the way to the volcano, **Naalehu** (population 2,173), bills itself as the southernmost community in the US (latitude 19° 3' 49" N). It has just enough space along the highway for a town theater, now a museum, across the street from a café and large Hawaiian sweet-bread factory.

A final southern detour worth making on the road to the volcano is off Ninole Loop at **Punaluu**. The **Punaluu Black Sands Beach Park** is one of the most beautiful in Hawaii. The lava sands are black, the palm trees are thick, and the rocky bay is often filled with hawksbill turtles, who lay their eggs on shore. Although the crashing waves appear too treacherous for swimming, the local people not only swim and surf here, but wade out and cast large fishing nets into the spray.

☞ Hawaii Volcanoes National Park

The Big Island's biggest attraction, the home of the fire goddess and land eater, Pele, is **Hawaii Volcanoes National Park** (Route 11, 30 miles (48 km) from Hilo, 96 miles (154 km) from Kona, open daily 24 hours a day, Tel. (808) 985-6000). A fee, good for 7 consecutive days, is collected at the gate.

Information is available inside the park at the **Kilauea Visitor Center** (open daily 7:45am–5pm), the **Thomas A. Jaggar Museum** (open daily 8:30am–5pm), and the **Volcano House Hotel**, founded on the crater rim in 1846. The great allure is that this is one of the most active volcanic regions on Earth. Mauna Loa erupted 14 times in the 20th century alone. The lower caldera, the one you can drive around, **Kilauea**, has been in continuous eruption since 1983, sending its molten lava streaming to the sea. The degree of actual volcanic activity (steam vents, bubbling lava pools) depends on whether the mountain is awake or dozing when you visit.

The Volcano House provides a fine overlook into the 2-mile (3-km) wide Kilauea crater. It was here that Mark Twain stayed in 1877, although most of the present structure dates from 1941 (the older Victorian-style building destroyed, appropriately, by fire). For closer views of the crater, you'll want to check in at the Visitors' Center, then explore the 11-mile (18 km) **Crater Rim Drive** encircling the caldera.

Don't miss the overlooks at **Halemaumau**, the crater that is home to Pele herself, which last erupted in 1982, and at **Kilauea Iki**, where the lava flows from a mighty 1959 eruption are still steaming. You can make a 2-hour (4-mile/6.4-km) hike across the floor of this crater from the overlook or take a

30-minute stroll on **Devastation Trail** through the cinder fall-out from that 1959 eruption. A third site worth parking the car for is the **Thurston Lava Tube**, a prehistoric cave in a forest of ferns that was once filled with lava.

Branching off from Crater Rim Drive is the even more dramatic **Chain of Craters Road**, which descends 20 miles (32 km) to the sea 3,700 ft (1,128 m) below, dead-ending where a 1995 lava flow buried the coastal highway. Many visitors head down to the sea just before sunset to view the red rivulets of fiery rock streaming down the hillside lava fields where it boils the seawater it meets and turns it into steam. At times it is possible to hike across the lava fields to see this phenomenon; check for current conditions with park rangers at the Visitors' Center. Whether or not there's much to see at sea level, this road is worth taking just for its views of the vast lava fields which have recently altered the face of the Big Island. Since 1986, nine miles (14 km)

Lava arches emerge from the water along the dramatic
Chain of Craters Road.

Exotic flowers abound in and around the historic town of Hilo.

of the coast road have been covered by lava. Flows erased an entire town from the map in 1960; drowned a park visitor center in 1989; and engulfed an important Hawaiian shrine, Wahaula Heiau, on the coast in 1997. Be especially careful crossing the seashore lava. The newly created shoreline is subject to collapse without warning. The most recent breakup, in 1999, dropped 20 acres (8 hectares) of bench lava into the sea.

Near Kilauea, the village of **Volcano**, tucked into the luxuriant tropical vegetation, is a sleepy Hawaiian town that has become a hideaway for artists, celebrities, and retirees. For the traveler, it now offers a handful of excellent cafés and fine bed-and-breakfast accommodations.

Hilo

It gets plenty of rain (over 130 inches/330 cm, some years), but that keeps **Hilo** green and resplendent. **Liliuokalani Gardens** sits right on the bay, a spacious Japanese design with pagodas and koi ponds. Nearby is **Banyan Drive**, where the big trees were planted by celebrities in the 1930s (each has a placard), from Ameila Earhart to Babe Ruth. The historic downtown is being restored and revitalized. There's an old park bandstand there; the **Pacific Tsumami Museum** (Hilo was hit hard by tidal waves in 1946 and 1960) is ensconced in a 1931 bank building; and the city's library is the setting for the 3.5-ton **Naha Stone** that Kamehameha the Great reputedly lifted to confirm prophecies of his rise to power. The **Lyman**

Museum and Mission House, also downtown, has a large collection of Hawaiian treasures, from seashells to an authentic early 19th-century missionary house.

South of Hilo is the **Puna** coast, a remote, largely undeveloped region where surfers and hippies often congregate. It can be a beautiful drive. **Lava Tree State Park** is filled with towering ohia trees and grotesque tree molds, formed when molten lava coated tree trunks and scoured out deep fissures in the tree roots. The **Isaac Hale Beach Park** is a local favorite for family swimming and surfing; the thermal pools nearby are used by locals as natural hot tubs. The road ends where recent lava flows stopped it in its tracks.

North of Hilo, nature both "rains" and reigns. The **Hawaii Tropical Botanical Garden** in Onomea is a rain-forest paradise with palm and mango groves and over 2,000 species of exotic and native plants. **Akaka Falls State Park** has a spectacular 420-ft (128-m) waterfall. The gem on the Hamakua Coast is the **Waipio Valley**, where the coastal highway ends (west of Kukuihaele). There's a superb overlook of the 2,000-ft- (610-m-) deep valley below, which was once home to 40,000 Hawaiians. The population is perhaps no more than 40 today, although there are scenic taro farms on the floor of this primeval valley, as well as the sites of ancient temples. Only four-wheel drive vehicles are allowed into this mysterious, fecund "Valley of the Kings," but the ambitious and fit can hike in and out over a steep, winding, one-way road.

KAUAI

The oldest and most northerly of the main islands, Kauai is rightly nicknamed "the Garden Isle." No island is more verdant, flowery, or scenic. Ripped apart in 1992 by hurricane Iniki, Kauai has replenished itself. It's an island of small towns, quiet and relaxed, a world apart from the more crowded and touristy portions of Oahu, Maui, and even the Big Island. The Poipu district to the south draws the most visitors, with its beaches, condos, and sunsets, while the North Coast is a fabled region of gardens and tiny roads, capped by the remote, roadless sea cliffs of the Na Pali Coast. The center of the island is the peak of Waialeale (5,240 ft/1,600 m), the volcano that formed Kauai. To the west lies Hawaii's greatest valley, Waimea Canyon, which lures most of Kauai's visitors, but the formal gardens and coastal backroads are just as spectacular.

Waimea Canyon

The southwestern shores of Kauai are where Captain Cook first landed on this island in 1778. There's a statue of the explorer, a copy of the one in his hometown in England, on the main street of Waimea town. The lava stone ruins of the Russian **Fort Elizabeth** lie near the mouth of the Waimea River, testimony to a brief military presence to enforce the Russian fur trade in the early 1800s. A bit farther up the river is evidence of an even older site, the **Menehune Ditch**, an ancient aqueduct (still functional) of fitted stonework, used to irrigate taro fields. Legends say it was dug in one night by the mythic *menehune,* the prodigious leprechauns of Hawaiian myth.

Along the road to the ditch is a strange, but arresting Buddhist temple, the **Waimea Shingon Mission**, which contains outdoor displays resembling rocket nose-cones. These feature the stone images of Buddha's followers that immigrants once posted in nearby mountains to recreate the 88 stations of a Japanese saint's pilgrimage. The images, dating from 1908, were moved to this mission in 1958.

One of Hawaii's best sugar plantation tours is at the **Gay & Robinson Sugar Visitor Center** just east of Waimea at Kaumakani. Tours, by reservation only (Monday–Friday 8:45am, 12:45pm), consist of a 2-hour ride through fields and the factory of a working sugar mill operation (harvest is April–October). Kauai's homegrown coffees can be sampled at the **Kauai Coffee Company**, with a small museum and gift shop, in nearby Eleele. The coastal highway ends north of Waimea at Polihale State Park, where you can view **Niihau Island**, a privately-owned, invitation-only isle, inhabited by a few hundred full-blooded Hawaiians committed to leading a traditional life. Owned by the Robinson family since 1864, the island's 200 or so residents work for its owners, rearing cattle and sheep, making charcoal from *kiawe* trees, gathering honey and making delicate necklaces strung with tiny rare shells.

Waimea Canyon, the "Grand Canyon of the Pacific," is just ten miles (16 km) long and 3,657 ft (1,115 m) deep at its deepest point, but it seems grand enough, and the cascading rock walls are as golden as those of mainland America's larger desert canyons. The road actually has only a few viewpoints, so take

When Mark Twain saw the vast Waimea Canyon, he dubbed it the "Grand Canyon of the Pacific."

advantage of the marked lookouts. Near the top, at **Kokee State Park**, there's an information center (the **Kokee Natural History Museum**, open daily 10am–4pm), restaurant, lodge, small plant garden, and usually a scattering of once-domesticated chickens, now wildfowl. The drive culminates at **Kalalau Valley Overlook** (elevation 4,120 ft/1,257 m) where there is a view not of the canyon, but of the even more spectacular Na Pali Coast and its largest valley. A hiking trail here leads east to the mountain peaks that are the wettest spots on earth.

Poipu

The south shore at **Poipu** (*Poipu* means "poi-pounder," referring to the pounding surf) is rife with condos and resorts, but the rural nature of life here still predominates. Whaling and sugarcane built up the area before vacationers arrived. **Poipu Beach** has Kauai's safest swimming beaches, with good snorkeling around the point to the west. **Koloa Town** has a refurbished 19th-century main street of galleries, cafés, and shops for tourists, built around a 1925 monkeypod tree and a small museum devoted to Ladd & Co, who opened the very first commercial sugarcane operation here in 1839. Other historical landmarks in the area are the **Koloa Church** with the tall white steeple, founded in 1835 by New England missionaries, and the **St. Raphael Church**, Kauai's oldest Catholic shrine (1854).

West of Poipu is **Spouting Horn**, where the surf spouts through lava tubes like a seaside Old Faithful. To the north is one of Hawaii's botanical gems, **Allerton & McBryde Gardens**, part of the National Tropical Botanical Garden. Queen Emma, wife of Kamehameha IV, vacationed on this sugarcane plantation estate, which was later transformed into a landscaped preserve for thousands of native plants and South Pacific fauna and flora never before seen in Hawaii. Guided tours of the 80-acre (32-hectare) gardens (Monday–Saturday

8:30am–5pm) and historic Allerton house are expensive, but delightful. Poipu is joined to the main southwest highway by a shady **Tunnel of Trees**, made up of eucalyptus called "swamp mahogany," planted in 1911 by a sugarcane baron.

Lihue, Wailua, & Kapaa

Visitors to Kauai arrive at **Lihue**, most by air, some by cruise liners docking at sheltered Nawiliwili Beach. Lihue is part small old town, part modern tourist center. The **Kauai Museum** (4428 Rice Street; Monday–Friday 9am–4pm, Saturday 10am–4pm, closed Sunday; admission fee; Tel: (808) 245-6931) in downtown Lihue has some fascinating artifacts, including tapa cloth, feather leis, poi bowls, and displays recounting the history of the island. **Grove Farm** (4050 Nawiliwili Road, Tel. (808) 245-3202), open on a limited basis for guided tours during the week, is a low-profile preserve of sugarcane plantation days.

North of Lihue, the east coast towns of **Wailua** and **Kapaa** have become top beach spots (once the private reserves of royal Hawaiians). Wailua is where the river boats, staffed with Hawaiian dancers and singers, head up to **Fern Grotto**, a jungle cave with primeval ferns. It's all a bit kitschy, much like the famous **Coconut Grove Hotel** near the mouth of the Wailua River, which is where Elvis Presley starred in *Blue Hawaii*. The hotel epitomized the faux Hawaiian experience for decades, until Hurricane Iniki closed it down in 1992. Ten years later it is making a return as a resort hotel. If you drive instead of sail up the Wailua River, you'll see plenty of small fern grottoes along the way, as well as an overlook for an ancient Hawaiian temple (Ka Lae O Ka Manu Heiau) and Kauai's **Opaekaa Falls**.

North Shore & Na Pali

Kauai's North Shore has just about every element required of a tropical island paradise, from beaches to gardens, combined

The old lighthouse at Kilauea Point National Wildlife Refuge, Kauai.

with a tiny population that lives life fully, but at a relaxed pace. It's a favorite getaway of celebrities, residents from other islands, and a few lucky travelers. **The Kilauea Point National Wildlife Refuge** underlines the beauty and remoteness of northern Kauai. The lighthouse on jutting seacliffs, built in 1913, is nestled next to a new visitors' center that concentrates on the abundant wildlife: red-footed boobies, Nene geese (the endangered state bird), Laysan albatross (gooney birds), porpoises, turtles, and whales.

Kilauea town is the site of the **Guava Kai Plantation** (open daily 9am–5pm) with free tours of its specimen garden and free tastes of guava juice and jams. Between Kilauea and Princeville, visitors can drive down to the sea for a look at the **Anini Beach** area, a reef-protected white sand shoreline of coves favored by swimmers, parasailers, windsurfers, and long-time Hawaii residents. This is among the least discovered and most beautiful vacation hideaways in the islands, where one can rent a beach cottage and disappear into sunny Hawaii for weeks or perhaps years.

Princeville, on the northern bluffs, is home to Kauai's most upscale resort, Princeville Hotel, and condo development. It overlooks **Hanalei Bay**, where the movie *South Pacific* was filmed.

To get closer, take the road on down to Hanalei itself. It's a road you won't soon forget, where one-lane wooden bridges cross taro fields and streams in a faraway valley that leads to the Na Pali coast. There are villages, old churches, and general stores along the way, and breathtaking beaches at every turn, including **Lumahai Beach, Tunnels**, and **Haena Beach** (the Bali Hai setting for *South Pacific*). Also near the end of the little road there's **Limahuli Garden and Preserve** (open Tuesday–Friday and Sunday 9:30am–4pm; admission fee; Tel. (808) 826-1053), a cliffside time-capsule of botanic Hawaii as it was in the days of the Polynesian settlers. Its lava rock terraces date back seven centuries. Don't expect bright blooming flowers; this is Hawaii as it was before Westerners introduced such plants.

Kee Beach is the end of the Kuhio Highway that crosses the North Shore. Swimming is good here, snorkeling can be excellent, and the sunsets are particularly worth driving out to see. This is where the fabled **Na Pali Coast** begins. There are no roads – just the **Kalalau Trail**. Many hikers attempt the first two miles (3.2 km) in and out of this steep trail as far as

Sunset at Kee Beach, where the Kuhio Highway ends, and the Na Pali Coast begins.

Hanakapiai Beach; a permit is required for hardy walkers to continue this challenging cliffside ramble its full 11 miles (18 km) to remote Kalalau, where you can pitch a tent. You'll have to hike back out, too, since there's no road or services at the end of the trail. Even highly experienced trekkers are surprised at the difficulty of this hike, but no one is disappointed by its sheer beauty. Charter boats and helicopters also rove along Na Pali, truly a land's end for Hawaii's tourists.

MOLOKAI

This is the island to visit to get away from it all. Oahu, the Big Island, Maui, and even Kauai are tourist-infested by comparison. Only on Molokai is the majority of the population (totaling under 7,000) native Hawaiian, and everything is truly rural. The cross-island two-lane highway is only about 38 miles (61 km) long (the island is just 10 miles/16 km wide); there isn't a single traffic light anywhere on Molokai; and even the number of rental cars is deliberately limited. The main town, Kaunakakai, is a page out of the 1920s, stretching for a few blocks, often nearly deserted. Farming and fishing are the chief industries. Much of the land was homesteaded in the 1920s. Yet Molokai offers more than just quietude, serene beauty, and native culture. Here you'll find Hawaii's longest beach, best mountain biking trails, a ranch resort with horseback riding, remote coastal valleys, the world's tallest seacliffs, and Father Damien's celebrated, isolated leper colony, still operating, with no road in or out, just a perilous seacliff trail up and down, which you can travel on a mule.

Molokai Ranch

The western end of the island is dominated by ranch lands. The former plantation town of **Maunaloa** has a kite factory, general store, theater, and **Molokai Ranch Lodge**, gateway to a

Papohaku Beach, the longest white-sand beach in Hawaii, is a highlight of Molokai.

vast ranch resort that offers over 50 eco-adventures, from mountain biking and horseback riding to sea kayaking on its distant beach (where spiffy, solar-powered "tentalows" are the accommodations). Once a safari park, **Molokai Ranch** has reverted to pastureland with a view of the rugged seashores.

The main highway begins and ends at the ranch. Spurs lead down to uncrowded **Papohaku Beach**, the longest white-sand beach in Hawaii (3 miles/5 km), good for swimming and beach-combing, and **Hale O Lono Harbor**, home of the hula in September during the annual Aloha Week and starting point of the **Molokai Hoe**, since 1952 the world's premier open-water outrigger canoe race (ending 41 miles/66 km later in Waikiki). Some consider Molokai the birthplace of the hula; you can see it at its traditional best, with ancient rites still performed, on Papohaku Beach in May at the Ka Hula Piko Festival.

Kaunakakai and Halawa Valley

You can lose yourself for days if you drive slowly enough ˴

Take in the incredible views amidst magnificent switch-backs on the road to Halawa Valley.

to east across Molokai's main two-lane (sometimes one-lane) highway. The main town is **Kaunakakai**, with its 1920s main street, hometown restaurants, and the 1925 **Kanemitsu Bakery** which, if you get there early enough, sells sweet, delectable breads and pastries. On the western edge of town, the **Kapuaiwa Coconut Grove** was planted by King Kamehameha V in the 1860s; this is one of Hawaii's only surviving royal groves.

North of town are two humble, very friendly attractions, the **Coffees of Hawaii** plantation store, where you can sample Molokai's only home-grown commercial coffees, and **Purdy's All-Natural Macadamia Nut Farm** (open daily 9am–3:30pm; Lihi Pali Avenue, Hoolehua), where the owner will crack the mysteries of this rich roasted nut that's become synonymous with Hawaii. While you're up this way, stop by the tiny **Hoolehua Post Office**, where the postmistress will be glad to help you address the coconuts in the bins there and send them on their way to those on the US mainland, all for the price of postage.

The road to **Halawa Valley** is Molokai's version of Maui's "Road to Hana." It's a shorter road, but it has its own magnificent switchbacks and beach scenery, with an Eden at the east end. The traffic is light, the drivers friendly, so you should be able to negotiate the one-lane bridges and narrow, bumpy sections. Along the way, stop off at the tiny **St. Joseph's Church**, built by Father Damien in 1876, and **Our Lady of Sorrows Church**, also built by Father Damien (1874), whose statue stands in the churchyard. Ancient Hawaiian fishponds, marked by lava rock breakers, can be seen all along the shore – in fact nowhere else in Hawaii are there so many of these fish farms, which were exclusively in royal hands for centuries. Beyond the 20-mile road marker, the road narrows considerably and twists through lush valleys.

With perseverance, one winds down to the end of the road, just past the picturesque Jersalema Hou Church (1948) at **Halawa Valley Country Park** (mile marker 28). Farmers and taro fishermen once occupied this coastal valley, but a 1946 tidal wave drove out most residents. The black sand beach here is magnificent, but the waves can be fierce.

Kalaupapa Leper Colony

Isolated from the rest of Molokai and the world by the tallest seacliffs on the planet, **Kalaupapa**, the leper colony founded by a Belgian priest, Father Damien, beginning in

St. Francis church is one of the many attractions in the leper colony of Kalaupapa.

1873, is one of the wonders of the Pacific. Since 1866, lepers had been unceremoniously dumped here by ships at the "Place of the Living Dead." Father Damien provided for these outcasts, building a town, hospital, and church; he succumbed to leprosy himself in 1889. Leprosy, now properly called Hansen's disease, has had a cure since the 1940s, and the town's population has dwindled over the years to a few score, who will live out their lives here. No new patients have been permitted since the 1970s. When the last resident of the village passes away, the town will become a park. Until then, visitors (age 16 and above) are permitted to visit the area, but only as a member of a group organized by Damien Tours.

While you can arrive by plane these days or hike the treacherous cliff trail (both as part of an organized tour), the most memorable descent is via the **Molokai Mule Ride** (100 Kalae Highway; open Monday-Saturday 8am, by reservation only; Tel. (800) 567-7750 or (808) 567-6088). Up to 16 riders brave the seacliffs, riding experienced (if stubborn) mules, who know the 1,975 steps and 26 switchbacks of the 3.1-mile (5-km) Pali Trail well. The mules descend 1,664 ft (504 m) to the beach in a little over an hour. Mule-riding is more strenuous than it appears, requiring strong legs, attention to the reins, and enough faith to overcome vertigo.

In the village of Kalaupapa, visitors are given a full tour by school bus and on foot, often conducted by resident and town sheriff Richard Marks. Most of the village is off-limits, in deference to its citizens, but you can visit the **Damien Monument**, a gift of English schoolchildren in 1893; the lovely **St. Francis Church**; the Arts & Craft Shop across the street; and the **Museum & Bookstore** (open Monday–Saturday, 10am–2pm). You might get a glimpse of a few of the residents as the tour bus circles town, especially as it passes **Elaine's Place**, the village bar since about 1916. In the past, this village had the reputation of consuming more beer per capita than anywhere else in Hawaii. It has been open to tourism since 1946; among famous guests were Robert Louis Stevenson (1889), Jack London (1907), Shirley Temple (1949), and Red Skelton (1955). Mule rides have been safely conducted since 1972.

Groups usually have lunch near the beach at **Kalawao**, then a tour of the **St. Philomena Church and Cemetery**, founded in 1872 and expanded by Father Damien. It was here that the original leper colony stood until 1895. While Father Damien's own grave is actually in Belgium (his exhumed body moved there in 1936), you'll find his Hawaiian grave and statue at this church (where his hand, sent from Belgium, is now entombed). An even older Christian shrine, the **Church of the Healing Spring (Siloama)**, founded by 35 patients of the Congregationalist faith in 1866, stands just up the road. After plenty of "talk story" at each stop, it's just a little over an hour back to civilization, unless you're still too saddle-sore to re-board your mule.

LANAI

Throughout most of the 20th century, Hawaii's "Pineapple Island" was the world's largest source of pineapple, a "plantation island" operated by the Dole Company (later Castle & Cooke, Inc.). Tourism was born only when the pineapple industry faltered. In 1990 and 1991, two luxury resort hotels opened, the Lodge at Koele at the center of the island and the Manele Bay Hotel on the south coast, each with its own world-class golf course. In 1993, commercial pineapple operations ceased completely. David Murdock of Castle & Cooke now owns 98% of Lanai, but you'll be hard-pressed to find a single pineapple field. Instead, you'll discover a small isle (13 miles (21 km) wide, 18 miles (29 km) long), with just 2,800 residents, 30 miles (48 km) of road, and one little 1920s town

– along with 47 miles (76 km) of coastline and white sand beaches, stunning tropical forests, fine restaurants, snorkeling coves with spinner dolphins, world-class golf links, sporting clays, and horseback-riding trails. You can have pretty much all of this to yourself. Just seven miles (11 km) offshore from Maui, Lanai is a world away. No other Hawaiian island approaches Lanai as a true tropical hideaway.

At the center of the island is **Lanai City**, built as a model company town for pineapple workers in 1924 by the Hawaiian Pineapple Company (later Dole Pineapple). Many of the quaint, rustic wood-frame structures remain intact. Restaurants, shops, stores, a theater, and a laundromat line the town square **Dole Park**, which has a fine stand of Cook Island pines planted half a century ago. Locals line up for the plate lunches here at the Blue Ginger Café. The Police Station at one corner of the square is especially quaint: Small portable shacks serve as the

The Lodge at Koele is the site of these splendid links, one of two world-class golf courses on Lanai.

On the island of Lanai, Hulopoe Bay is the ideal place to explore exquisite tide pools.

cells of the city jail. Above the square is the 11-room **Hotel Lanai**, built in 1923 to entertain guests and Dole Company executives. It is now the evening gathering place of tourists and locals for dinner and "talk story" sessions on the veranda.

The **Lodge at Koele** is located just beyond Lanai City, near the riding stables. It resembles an elegant English manor, but its library has many volumes on Hawaii. The landscaped grounds have spacious areas for lawn bowling and croquet, and the golf course, designed by Greg Norman and Ted Robinson, is championship class. Many, if not most, of Lanai's visitors come to play golf – and Lanai City obliges with the Cavendish Golf Course, its own 9-hole layout, free to all residents (visitors are urged to leave a donation).

Lanai's other big resort, **Manele Bay Hotel**, is a more typical, splendid beachside complex with beautiful gardens, plush swimming pools, and its own golf course, designed by Jack

☞ Nicklaus. Its location on **Hulopoe Bay** is superb, because it's here that you'll find the island's best swimming, snorkeling, and tide pools. Here, schools of spinner dolphins regularly sweep through to sport with those lucky enough to be in the water. At the extreme southern point of the bay is the rock island of **Puupehe**; it recalls the legend of a maiden kept in a sea cave here by her jealous husband until she was drowned by the stormy surf.

Most of Lanai is remote and serene, and was never planted for pineapple or any other crop. The isle is fascinating to explore, but most roads require four-wheel-drive transportation. You can rent these vehicles yourself or hire a local driver/guide to take you around for the day. The **Munro Trail**, beginning one mile north of Lanai City, is a seven-mile (11-km) dirt road rising through rain forests to the summit of **Lanai Hale Mountain** (3,370 ft/1,027 m), where on a clear day you can see six other Hawaiian islands. This ridge was planted with Cook Island pine, ironwood, and eucalyptus decades ago by ranch manager George Munro, who hoped to draw moisture from the passing clouds. (Today, half of Lanai's water comes from "fog drip," with each large pine at the summit catching 250 gallons per hour.)

From the heights of the Munro Trail (which hikers as well as four-wheelers follow), you can descend on back roads to **Shipwreck Beach**, where there's still the concrete hull of a World War II Liberty ship caught on the reef. The beach, with Maui in the background, is often deserted; the beachcombing extends for miles (watch for glass balls freed from fishing nets). A few miles southwest of the shipwreck is **Keomuku**, a sugarcane boom town of 2,000 people that became a ghost town overnight.

Six miles (10 km) northwest of Lanai City, at **Kanepuu**, is the **Native Hawaiian Dryland Forest**, 590 acres (239 hectares) under the stewardship of the Nature Conservancy. A self-guided loop trail with signage takes visitors through the largest remains of native olive and ebony (*olopua* and *lama*) dryland forests in Hawaii. There are also 48 plant species unique to Hawaii here, including endangered gardenia (*nau*) and sandalwood (*ilihai*).

Bordering this preserve, at the end of Polihua Road, are Lanai's badlands, the **Garden of the Gods** (so named by George Munro), where the red rocks and purple lava formations have been carved by wind and sea spray into a celestial landscape of eerie pinnacles. One of the least-visited sites on the island is the ancient fishing village of **Kaunolu** on the southwest coast. The sea cliffs are filled with the remains of ancient temples, homes, and graves; the shoreline offers good snorkeling and secluded sunbathing. This was Kamehameha the Great's favorite fishing spot, his ultimate recreational getaway, as it still is for a few modern travelers two centuries later.

The Garden of the Gods, Lanai's badlands, offer a strange expanse of bizarre land formations.

Hawaii's Other Islands

Visitors usually confine their travels to the four main Hawaiian islands – Oahu, Maui, Kauai, and the Big Island of Hawaii. Some travelers add Molokai and Lanai to their itineraries. No discussion of Hawaii would be complete, however, without mentioning some other islands in the chain.

Niihau. Just 17 miles (27 km) from Kauai, the 73-sq mile (189-sq km) island of Niihau (nee-ee-how) is called "The Forbidden Island" because it is privately owned and cannot be visited without an invitation from one of the 225 inhabitants. Most of the residents are pure-blooded Hawaiians who speak the language. The men are engaged in ranching operations for Bruce Robinson, owner of the island; the women collect and string the tiny Niihau seashells into delicate necklaces that fetch big prices. There are no hotels on Niihau – nor electricity or running water. Once they finish the lower grades, the children of Niihau attend school on Kauai. Niihau's people are free to leave the island, but once they move elsewhere for extended periods, they may be refused permission to return.

Kahoolawe. Barren Kahoolawe (kah-ho-oh-law-vay) is a tiny island just off the southwest coast of Maui. Once inhabited by ancient Hawaiians, the island has since served as an Alcatraz for criminals, a cattle ranch, and – most recently – a bombing range for the U.S. Navy (1939 to 1990). Now turned back to the state, the island is littered with unexploded bombs. Clean-up is slow and expensive, but plans call for Kahoolawe to become a cultural reserve. Until then, it remains essentially off-limits to the public.

Midway. Lying some 1,100 miles northwest of Honolulu, Midway is an atoll comprising a few tiny islands. Best known as the site of a pivotal World War II battle in the Pacific, Midway Islands is no longer a military base but is open to the public, managed by the U.S. Fish & Wildlife Department as a refuge for the millions of Laysan Albatross (called gooney birds for their comical awkwardness at takeoff and landing) who nest there. Aloha Airlines offers scheduled flights to Midway. For more information, contact Midway-Phoenix (Tel. (888) 643-9291; fax (770) 386-3053; <www.midwayisland.com>).

WHAT TO DO

In Hawaii, the beach is the center of a galaxy of activities, from beach-combing to surfing. Many of the land activities, from shopping to golf, draw on the seascape as well. Whatever you're doing outdoors, protect yourself from the sun's ultra-violet rays with a sunscreen or cream with a high protection factor (SPF). If you play in the water, reapply sunblock. Wherever you go in the sun, wear a hat and sunglasses, too. If you're tanning, expose yourself to the sun for short intervals. Hawaii lies near enough to the equator that its rays are probably more intense than you're used to at home.

BEACH SPORTS

Conditions on Hawaii's many splendid beaches vary greatly with season, location, tides, and ocean conditions. Winter generally brings higher, more dangerous waves and undertows. Check with locals or lifeguards before taking the plunge.

Waikiki's Kuhio Beach is a perfect location for a family outing of swimming, sunbathing, and even surfing.

Swimming. Starting at Oahu's Waikiki Beach, swimming along Hawaii's warm shores is a pleasure. There are calm waters for swimmers of all ages at Lanikai Beach and Ala Moana Beach on Oahu. Top swimming spots on Maui are at Kaanapali Beach and Kapalua Beach, a family favorite. Big Island swimmers can enjoy Kekaha Kai State Park, the lagoons at Leleiwi Beach near Hilo, and picture-perfect Kaunaoa Beach at the Mauna Kea Resort. Kee Beach at the start of the Na Pali Coast, Anini Beach, and Kalapaki Beach, a hidden gem at the Marriott Resort in Lihue, offer good swimming on Kauai. Swimmers on Molokai will find safe waves on Sandy Beach.

Snorkeling. Mask, fins, and snorkel open a wonderland just below the surface at many of Hawaii's beaches, where coral reefs, green sea turtles, and schools of colorful fish congregate. Dive shops such as Snorkel Bob's rent equipment inexpensively by the day or for the week. Legendary snorkeling spots include Hanauma Bay on Oahu, Molokini off Maui (which requires signing up for a snorkel cruise), and Kealakekua Bay, a Marine Sanctuary near Captain Cook's Landing on the Big Island. Lanikai Beach is another favorite spot on Oahu, while Maui visitors flock to Kapalua Beach near Napili, Black Rock at Kaanapali Beach, and Ulua Beach at Wailea. The Big Island offers superb snorkeling in a turtle-infested cove at the end of Hapuna Beach, easy snorkeling at Kahaluu Beach on the Kona Coast, and still more turtles at Anaehoomalu Bay in front of the Outrigger Waikoloa Beach Hotel. The Poipu beaches, Kee Beach, and the gentle Anini Beach areas draw snorkelers on Kauai, while there are often spinner dolphins to cavort with at Hulopoe Beach on Lanai.

SCUBA Diving. Divers, who must be certified, can get lessons and equipment, as well as charter dive cruises on all the islands. Oahu's best dives are offshore, at spots like Kahuna Canyon and at the wreck of the Mahi off Waianae. Maui divers like the

Makena Coast and Molokini. There are manta rays, dolphins, turtles, and octopuses off the Kona Coast on the Big Island, especially in Kealakekua Bay. Divers flock to the Caverns beyond Kauai's Poipu shores. Lanai dive spots include the undersea Cathedrals I and II.

Bodysurfing & Boogie Boarding. A good place to learn and practice riding the waves is at Waikiki Beach. Experienced bodysurfers take on the surf at Oahu's Makapuu Beach or at Sandy Beach, where the waters are quite dangerous (there are more rescues here than at any other beach!). Hapuna Beach on the Big Island is another great place to bodysurf or try a boogie board.

Windsurfing. Many of Hawaii's windswept beaches and coves are ideal for windsurfing. Kailua Beach is Oahu's best place to learn; the same can be said for Anini Beach on Kauai. Maui boasts some of the finest windsurfing in the islands at Hookipa Beach Park, on the road to Hana, and at Kihea, too. Those who want to fly above the waves by parasailing can charter the boat and equipment at Waikiki or along Kaanapali Beach on Maui.

Kayaking & Canoeing. Sea kayaking is especially popular at Lanikai Beach and Kailua Beach on Oahu, the Kihei Coast and Hana on Maui, and at Molokai Ranch on Molokai island. Kayakers and canoeists can rent vessels and row along the shores of Poipu or the remote Na Pali Coast on Kauai, where you can also

Anini Beach on Kauai offers ideal conditions for the challenge of windsurfing.

Surfers make statements of style riding the waves or just strolling the sands of Hawaii.

tackle the Huleia River or row up the wide Wailua River to the Fern Grotto.

Fishing. You can cast from shore at some of Hawaii's beach parks or go charter fishing offshore on nearly all of Hawaii's islands. The blue marlin is the trophy fish in these waters; tuna, ono, and swordfish are also abundant. Charter fishing boats, many of which practice tag-and-release fishing, leave from Kewalo Basin on Oahu, the Kona coast on the Big Island, and from Lahaina and Maalaea Harbor on Maui. No license is required for charter fishing.

Beachcombing. You won't find many unbroken shells on Hawaii's shores, but the tidal pools and sunsets are marvelous on a number of gorgeous beaches. Strollers love Oahu's north shore and Ko Olina's lagoons on the west coast, Kauai's Hanalei Beach, Anini Beach, and Mahaulepu Beach, Molokai's long Papohaku Beach, and the tide pools at Hulupoe and Shipwreck Beaches on Lanai.

Another popular watersport in Hawaii is whale-watching (from shore or aboard whale cruises). Humpback whales make these waters their winter home, usually from December through April. Snorkeling, sunset cruises, and glass-bottom boat sea tours are available on many major piers. Small submarines provide brief scenic dives off Waikiki and Lahaina.

Surfing

Hawaii is the birthplace of surfing. You can learn to surf in as little as a few hours at some of the beaches, where instruction and board rentals are available, particularly along Waikiki Beach. You can also challenge world-class waves, especially in the winter, or just watch the pros practice and compete. While Waikiki is perfect for beginners, Oahu's Sandy Beach is for daredevils, and the giant waves on the North Shore, at Waimea Beach, Sunset Beach, and the Banzai Pipeline attract the world's most skilled wave riders. The Big Island requires experienced surfers, who hang out along the Kona Coast and the Puna beaches south of Hilo. Maui has some gentle surfing spots in the summer, but the winter waves are more challenging, especially at Hookipa Beach and Honolua Bay. Murphy Beach Park in Molokai can be a place for novices to practice, but only in the summer.

In addition to "discovering" Hawaii in 1778, Captain Cook discovered "surfing" on the same voyage. The ancient Hawaiians had been surfing for centuries, of course, purely for the excitement. They probably invented it upon arrival in these islands, where the surf, unimpeded by nearby land masses, strikes Hawaii with those big perfect waves. Until modern times, Hawaiian surfers relied on boards up to 6 ft (1.8 m) long, except for those of royal blood, who were privileged to ride boards up to 16 ft (5 m) long (better for the larger waves). Missionaries later regarded surfing as a waste of time, and it fell out of favor until the 1880s, when the "Merry Monarch" brought it back into fashion. Americans started surfing not in Southern California, but at Waikiki's Outrigger Canoe Club in 1908. The King of the Surfers, as well as an Olympic gold medallist in swimming, Duke Kahanamoku (1890–1968) was the modern master of the heavy 16-ft surfboard. His statue stands at Waikiki's Kuhio Beach today, where he grew up surfing. Today's surfboards, made of a special foam and equipped with a skeg are shorter (about 9 ft/2.7 m) and far lighter than the ancient wooden models, and today's competitions are more fierce than playful. The world's greatest surfers still come to where it all started in Hawaii to compete, perform, and enjoy the island's waves, making surfing a top spectator sport as well.

LAND SPORTS

Hiking has a special appeal in Hawaii. Not only are there spectacular rain-forests and remote sea cliffs to trek, there are also no patches of poison ivy or snakes to worry about. There are plenty of trails on every island, and few if any are crowded (unlike some of the beaches). Oahu has over 30 major hiking trails, from the Diamond Head Crater trail, which can be done in as little as 90 minutes, to the Pali Trail, which traces the Koolau Mountain Range 11 miles north to Waimanalao Village. Another 11-mile trail (each way), Hawaii's most famous and one of the more challenging anywhere, is the trail along the roadless Na Pali Coast, although most hikers

Cyclists have plenty of ground to cover in Hawaii.

are quite satisfied with just the first two miles of ocean vistas. Another lesser known but pretty 11-mile hike is along the Munro Trail at the center of Lanai. On Molokai, the Pepeopae Trail has great views, but the hike down to the Kalaupapa leper colony (permit required) is the most unusual. There are excellent trails of varying lengths and elevations in Hawaii Volcanoes National Park on the Big

Horseback riders have a choice of terrain to explore.

Island and at Haleakala National Park on Maui. The trails through Waimea Canyon and at Kokee State Park on Kauai are grand. Permits are required for some of these hikes, so check with Parks offices on the appropriate island.

Camping often requires a permit, reservation, or fee in Hawaii's parks. In Hawaii you can set up a tent and play on the beach at many places, including Malaekahana Bay State Recreational Area on Oahu's North Shore, at Hulopoe Beach Park on Lanai, at Papohaku Beach, and at Polihale State Park on Kauai, the westernmost beach in the US. You can also find upscale camping at the Molokai Ranch's seaside tentalows, "spa" camping near natural pools and waterfall campsites at Oheo on Maui, lush valley camping in the Waipio Valley on the Big Island, garden camping at Hoomaluhia Botanical Gardens on Oahu, and "stellar" camping under the stars atop a volcano in Haleakala National Park on Maui.

Mountain bikers can rent bicycles and explore Molokai Ranch. Bicyclists can also coast for miles down the big volcano's slopes in Maui.

Hawaii's outdoors also beckons horseback riders. On Oahu, you can horseback ride on the beach at the Turtle Bay Resort. On Kauai, you can set out for the beach or cliffs on horseback from Princeville or Koloa. Equestrians on Maui can enjoy the Mendes Ranch or ride into the Kaleakala Crater. The stables at Koele on Lanai offer visitors an alternative to four-wheel vehicles, while at the Parker Ranch on the Big Island or at Molokai Ranch on Molokai, you can pretend you're a *paniolo* (Hawaiian cowboy) for a few hours while riding the great expanse of a working cattle ranch. Hawaiian visitors can also stand tall in the saddle of a mule, not only when visiting the isolated leper colony on Molokai, but when exploring the rugged Pololu Valley on the Big Island from Puu-O-Hoku Ranch.

Golf

A significant number of Hawaii's visitors come first and foremost to golf. The courses are breathtakingly beautiful, artful mixtures of lava, seacliff, and white sand. Many courses are owned by or linked to hotel resorts. The designers are topnotch, from Robert Trent Jones to Jack Nicklaus, and virtually all of the world's top golfers have played here. The courses are often crowded; midweek tee-times are best.

Oahu has a few top courses, including the 18-hole and 9-hole layouts at Turtle Bay Resort and the Sheraton Makaha Golf Club, but the neighboring islands really excel on the fairway front. Kauai boasts of its Poipu Bay Resort Golf Course, which has hosted the PGA Grand Slam of Golf, while the Kauai Lagoons and Princeville layouts are superb. Maui golfers have a choice of three wonderful seaside courses at Wailea Resort alone, while the resort layouts at Kapalua, Kaanapali, and Makena are very fine, too. The Big Island has some legendary links, including the venerable Mauna Kea course, the ecologically-friendly courses at Hapuna, and the graceful Hualalai Golf

Course, one of Jack Nicklaus's designs. Tiny Lanai has its big courses: The seaside Experience at Koele and the upcountry Challenge at Manele are one of the reasons tourism works there.

Spectator Sports

Hawaii is the place to play, rather than watch, sports. The major US professional sports leagues are not represented in Hawaii, but Hawaii's golf courses are frequently the setting for major tournaments, including PGA and Senior PGA events. Hawaii's best college teams are often those in volleyball (men's and women's) or basketball. What Hawaii offers the spectator are sports not seen much on the US mainland, such as outrigger canoe racing, windsurfing competitions, and world surfing championships in the winter.

SHOPPING

Hawaii has the same shopping opportunities that the US mainland provides. The big discount chains (Kmart, Wal-Mart, Costco, Safeway) have arrived on many of the islands, but prices are noticeably higher, owing to Hawaii's remote location. Most urban areas have shopping malls, with some interesting Hawaii-influenced shops and kiosks, and there are island towns lined with fascinating handicraft shops, boutiques, jewelers, galleries, dive shops, and T-shirt outlets. Hawaii has its own chains of convenience stores, such as the ubiquitous ABC shops, handy for picking up sundries, snacks, beach necessities, and loads of inexpensive souvenirs.

Honolulu has three main shopping centers with good selections of clothing and gifts: Ala Moana Center (over 200 outlets), the remodeled Aloha Tower Marketplace (where the cruise ships tie up), and the adjacent Ward Warehouse and newer Ward Center. Waikiki has the most shops for tourists, including the lavish DFS Galleria Shopping Center with its own aquarium and an interior modeled after the hull of a classic cruise liner. Honolulu is also the site of the Aloha Flea Market (Aloha Stadium, Wednesday, Saturday, and Sunday, 6am–3pm), with over 1,000 vendors selling collectibles – go as early as possible. Honolulu's Chinatown is one of the most intriguing places to browse and shop. There, on Maunakea Street, you'll find some of the best lei shops (their fresh flower wreathes are reasonably priced and can be shipped overseas) and stores featuring traditional Hawaiian fashions.

The bright Hawaiian print shirts, muumuu dresses, and sarongs are everywhere, and the longer you stay in Hawaii, the more irresistible they become. High quality and "antique" Aloha shirts are expensive, but can be worth the price; they usually qualify as business attire throughout the islands. More contemporary Hawaiian apparel is sold in leading local boutiques,

such as Sig Zane Designs. High-quality local handicrafts, using materials at hand such as taro leaves and koa wood, are harder to find. Most souvenir and department stores carry tawdry versions, often produced elsewhere. Hand-stitched Hawaiian quilts, introduced by the missionaries but wonderfully developed by native artists, can fetch high prices indeed. Perhaps the best place to seek

Honolulu's Chinatown is the place to shop for fresh leis and necklaces.

Familiar Hawaiian prints brighten up a variety of muumuus in this Honolulu shop window.

out handmade native goods is at museum shops (try the Honolulu Academy of Arts, the Contemporary Art Museum, or the Bishop Museum in Honolulu; the Kauai Museum in Kauai). A hui (group) of local artists in Oahu sells unique works at several "Native Books & Beautiful Things" outlets.

Many visitors buy art in Hawaii, and there are plenty of galleries with original work by local artists. Lahaina, Kihei, Wailuku, and Paia are known as gallery towns on Maui; so is Hanapepe town on Kauai. Lahaina and tiny Paia are quaint towns made for window shopping on Maui, as is Old Koloa Town on Kauai. Shopping on the Big Island is concentrated on Alii Drive in Kailua-Kona and at resort shopping centers, such as King's Shops on the Kohala Coast. A store called Hula Heaven at the Kona Inn Shopping Center features Hawaiian collectibles and even a Hawaiian Shirt Museum; half their goods are vintage, half are new but traditionally-styled.

Calendar of Events

JANUARY Ala Wai Challenge Canoe Festival (Waikiki, Oahu), outrigger races, traditional Hawaiian games; Chinese New Year Celebrations (Honolulu, Oahu), fireworks, food, and dragon dances in Chinatown (sometimes in February); Ka Molokai Makahiki (Kaunakakai, Molokai), Hawaiian games and sports, arts and crafts.

FEBRUARY NFL Pro Bowl (Honolulu, Oahu), all-star game in Aloha Stadium; Big Board Classic (Makaha, Oahu), surfing contest (sometimes in March); Punahou School Carnival (Honolulu, Oahu), a benefit for the scholarship fund; Waimea Town Celebration (Waimea, Kauai), top entertainment, sports, and food.

MARCH Oahu Kite Festival (Waikiki, Oahu), in Kapiolani Park; Prince Kuhio Celebration (all the islands, especially in Lihue, Kauai), parades and pageantry; Honolulu Festival (Waikiki, Oahu), Japanese plays, sumo, kite-making.

APRIL Merry Monarch Hula Festival (Hilo, Big Island), Hawaii's biggest hula competition; Celebration of the Arts (Kapalua, Maui), hands-on demonstrations of contemporary and traditional crafts; Hawaiian Slack Key Guitar Festival (Kailua-Kona, Big Island); Easter Sunrise Service (Honolulu, Oahu), at the National Cemetery of the Pacific in Punchbowl Crater.

MAY Lei Day (all the islands), lei-making, arts and crafts, music; Oceanfest (various locations, Oahu), surfing, swimming, and other ocean-based competitions; Prince Albert Music Festival (Princeville, Kauai), classical and Hawaiian music.

JUNE King Kamehameha Celebration (all the islands), lei draping on statues, floral parades, parties; Taste of Honolulu (Honolulu, Oahu), tastings of wine, beer, and tidbits from over 30 restaurants; King Kamehameha Hula Competition (Honolulu, Oahu), 500 dancers compete; Ka Lima O Maui (Wailea, Maui), 100 holes of golf, played from sunup to sundown.

JULY Prince Lot Hula Festival (Honolulu, Oahu), non-competitive hula celebration at Moanalua Gardens; Turtle Independence Day Celebration (Kohala Coast, Big Island), young green sea turtles raised at the Mauna Lani Resort set off to sea; Hawaii International Jazz Festival (Honolulu, Oahu); Pineapple Festival (Hulopoe Beach, Lanai), pineapple eating contest, cooking demo; Ukulele Festival (Waikiki, Oahu); Cuisines of the Sun (Kohala Coast, Big Island), food-lovers' fest.

AUGUST Hawaiian International Billfish Festival (Kailua-Kona, Big Island), big game fishing; Queen Liliuokalani Keiki Hula Competition (Honolulu, Oahu), with 500 children.

SEPTEMBER Aloha Festivals (all the islands), parades and street parties begin on Oahu and move on to the other islands during the

The Kodak Hula Show goes year-round on Waikiki.

next six weeks; Na Wahine O Ke Kai (Waikiki, Oahu), women's world outrigger canoe championships; Sam Choy Poke Recipe Contest (Kohala Coast, Big Island), marinated raw fish with seaweed, at its best.

OCTOBER Molokai Hoe (Waikiki, Oahu), annual men's outrigger canoe championship ends in Waikiki; Princess Kaiulani Keiki Hula Festival (Waikiki, Oahu), for kids ages 5 through 12; French Festival (Waikiki and Honolulu, Oahu), Hawaii dons a beret; Ironman Triathlon World Championship (Kailua-Kona, Big Island), grueling swim-bike-run; Terry Fox Cancer Research Benefit (Wailea, Maui), run in the sun for a good cause; Halloween in Lahaina (Lahaina, Maui), 30,000 ghosts and goblins haunt Front Street.

NOVEMBER World Invitational Hula Festival (Waikiki, Oahu); Kona Coffee Cultural Festival (Kailua-Kona, Big Island), pageants, parades, coffee-picking contest; Hawaii International Film Festival (various locations, Oahu and other islands); Winter Wine Escape (Kohala Coast, Big Island); top winemakers, top chefs; Triple Crown of Surfing (North Shore, Oahu), top surfers compete for big money.

DECEMBER Honolulu Marathon (Waikiki, Oahu), with 30,000 runners; Pacific Handcrafters Guild Christmas Fair (Honolulu, Oahu); Jingle Bell Run (Honolulu, Oahu), fun run with costumes and Christmas carols; Maui Marathon (West Maui), formerly in the spring.

For authentic contemporary treasures of the islands, keep an eye out for vendors at tourist sites. Their woven mats and baskets, created on the spot, are superb handicrafts. Local coffees, macadamia candies, taro treats, pineapples, and other edibles can be purchased nearly anywhere, from convenience stores to the airport, although savvy shoppers find the best selections at farm and plantation outlets.

ENTERTAINMENT

Honolulu, like other major US cities, has first-run films, concerts, nightclubs, bars, and festive celebrations, but unlike other American cities it also has Hawaiian and Polynesian entertainment. Some resort hotels, such as Hilton Hawaiian Village on Waikiki and the Outrigger Waikaloa Beach Hotel on the Big Island, have nightly variety shows featuring hula dancers and other traditional performers. For a free version of such performances, the Kodak Hula Show in the Waikiki area is still going strong. Hula shows, like the Polynesian variety shows, complete with buffets and fire dancers, are held regularly in several Waikiki hotels. They are spectacles designed for visitors that maximize the showy aspects of traditional entertainment forms. The dancers and singers performing at the Polynesian Cultural Center on Oahu are a bit more traditional than those entertaining visitors in Waikiki, but authentic hula is best enjoyed at annual festivals and competitions held throughout the islands, or at the hula demonstrations held in the Bishop Museum.

> Hawaiians, especially outside of Honolulu, are "laid back," so that "Hawaiian time" takes into account a measure of tardiness.

While there's been a strong movement to preserve and restore Hawaiian traditions and entertainment, hotel supper clubs and lounges often specialize in enhancing the romantic or nos-

The summit o f the Mount Haleakala volcano is down-right dizzying for those hardy hikers who reach it.

talgic image of Old Hawaii. Supper clubs in Waikiki are often headlined by Las Vegas-style acts with a Hawaiian twist or two, with singers following in the footsteps of the venerable Don Ho (of "Tiny Bubbles" fame). Some hotel bars, even in Waikiki, are more serene, such as the Halekulani's "House Without A Key," a lounge noted for its sunsets and hula shows.

Traditional Hawaiian musicians are much sought-after these days. These small "folk" groups play many venues, from resort lobbies and bars to shopping malls, airports, and performance centers. While their percussion instruments may be Hawaiian in origin, the ukulele and the slack-string guitar, synonymous with authentic Hawaiian folk music, are not, introduced by immigrants over the past two centuries.

Hawaii also has classical and contemporary entertainment, supplied by resident opera, theater, ballet, and dance companies. The Honolulu Symphony Orchestra performs regularly, as do international groups and celebrities. Nor is culture confined to Honolulu; the Visiting Artists Program, usually held monthly, brings renowned writers, actors, performers, and lecturers to the Lodge at Manele Bay on Lanai.

For many visitors, Hawaii's best entertainment after dark is provided by a sunset cruise, with dinner, drinks, or both – and almost always enhanced by warm breezes, gorgeous coastlines, and intense starlight.

HAWAII FOR CHILDREN

Hawaii is a natural playground for children on vacation. From volcanoes to beaches, boogie boards to smorgasbords, children from tots to teenagers usually find more to do on a vacation in Hawaii than nearly anywhere else. It's a natural Disneyland, with most youthful activities concentrated on the beaches or in the surf. From Kuhio Beach on Waikiki to Kahaluu Beach on the Big Island, there are many protected coves that have calm waters and shallow, stand-up depths, ideal for kids to wade or learn to ride the waves.

Honolulu has the most attractions geared to kids. The Honolulu Zoo and Waikiki Aquarium put on special shows for children. Sea Life Park has plenty of entertainment, including a water performance starring the world's only half-dolphin, half-whale. The Polynesian Cultural Center up-island offers a chance to learn Polynesian games, traditional bowling, and Pacific island dancing. Waikiki remains one of the best places in the world for children to learn boogie boarding and surfing.

The big resorts on Oahu and the neighboring islands usually have an array of special children-only programs that are both fun and educational, but it often turns out that parents and their children enjoy the same attractions and activities, such as submarine rides, snorkel dives, horseback trips, plantation tours, and lava field hikes.

EATING OUT

Hawaii was widely regarded as a culinary backwater until a dozen younger chefs launched the Hawaiian Regional Cuisine (HRC) movement, which had its formal birth in 1991. Today, food critics and gourmets talk up Hawaii as the ultimate meeting place of East-West eating traditions. For the leaders of the Hawaiian Regional Cuisine movement, including Roy Yamaguchi, Alan Wong, Sam Choy, Roger Dikon, Beverly Gannon, and Peter Merriman (all chefs with international followings), the crucial differences are the emergence of fresh ingredients supplied by local farmers and fishermen and the rise to prominence of distinctly Hawaiian dishes.

Hawaiian cooking employs a mixture of the ethnic traditions that make up the islands. The result is often called fusion food or Pacific Rim cuisine (chef Roy Yamaguchi calls it food with a "contemporary Euro-Asian cooking style"); by whatever name, its multi-ethnic dishes with fresh local ingredients have put Hawaii on the crest of a cooking wave sweeping the world.

Outdoor Sunday brunch is a full-sensory experience at the historic Moana Surfrider.

A menu at a top fusion restaurant in Hawaii today might include taro crab cakes, Maui onion soup, Waipio Valley fern shoots, Molokai sweet potatoes, and ahi spring rolls.

You don't have to pay top prices at the restaurants of star chefs to enjoy foods with a Hawaiian difference. While Italian restaurants, pizza places, steak houses, and all the world's fast-food chains abound, you can also count on Hawaiian cafés to

Fish of the Day

Menus always give the Hawaiian name for seafood, but sometimes neglect to translate. Here's what you're getting:

au	marlin (a Hawaiian term for any variety of marlin)
ahi	tuna (yellowfin or bigeye types)
aku	tuna (skipjack variety)
ehu	red snapper
hapuupuu	grouper (a type of sea bass)
hebi	spearfish
kajiki	blue marlin
kumu	goatfish
mahimahi	dorado (a dolphinfish, not related to the dolphin mammal)
nairagi	striped marlin
ono	wahoo (a type of mackerel)
opah	moonfish
opakapaka	pink snapper
tombo	albacore tuna
uhu	parrot fish
uku	gray snapper
ulua	jackfish

Note: The most common seafood on most menus are ahi, kajiki, mahimahi, ono, opakapaka, and tombo.

specialize in the exceptional seafood of the Pacific. Some experts regard the seafood of Hawaii as easily the best in the world.

Probably the most popular expression of Hawaiian cuisine among the people is the plate lunch. Ordered from lunch wagons, restaurant counters, and café windows, the plate lunch is built around "two scoops rice" served with fried seafood, teriyaki beef, or shoyu chicken. Sides

Fresh produce is prodigious in Hawaii's outdoor markets.

of macaroni salad or cole slaw are mandatory, as is a paper plate. Gravy is often ladled on, accompanied by a soft drink in a paper cup. If a Hawaiian plate lunch strikes you as excessive, consider another local institution, the loco moco: its three layers are rice, a hamburger, and two fried eggs, coated with brown gravy. These meals are derived from Hawaii's various immigrant populations who labored on plantations and ate heartily. The Japanese Hawaiian version is bento, a meal-in-a-box consisting of rice, pickled vegetables, and fried chicken, pork, or beef.

The longer you eat in Hawaii, the more local foods, treats, and dishes you're likely to come across. A popular dim sum-like snack is manapua, a doughy roll stuffed with beans or pork. Saimin is a bowl or cup of noodles in broth with scrambled eggs, green onions, and sometimes pork. Poke is raw fish, cubed and seasoned with onions and seaweed. Maui onions are the sweet, moist local rival of the Vidalia and Walla Walla onions of the US mainland. Hawaiian sweet bread is actually a Portuguese import, introduced in the late 19th century – soft, sweet bread that's become an island staple. The irresistibly-buttery macadamia nuts, introduced from Australia, became a cash crop in the 1930s, thriving in the Big Island's volcanic soil and rainfall; Hawaii now produces 90% of the world's supply.

Three of Hawaii's foods merit special mention. Malasadas are yeasty, holeless doughnuts which must be eaten while fresh and hot (another Portuguese import). Shave ice is the legendary snow cone of Hawaii, an absolute must if you visit Oahu's North Shore. Ice is shaved from a block, scooped into a paper cone, and saturated with colorful and sweet fruit syrups. Try the lilikoi (passion fruit) syrup. A third staple for many Hawaiians is neither native nor ethnic – it's Spam, the processed luncheon meat in a can that was popular once-upon-a-time during and after World War II all over America. Only Hawaiians remained loyal to Spam in the decades since; try it fried for dinner.

You might have a chance to sample some of the ethnically Hawaiian foods and dishes at a luau. A luau is a festive banquet that dates from early tribal days when people got together to celebrate a wedding, birthday, or family reunion, invoking the blessings of the gods. The centerpiece of a luau these days is Kalua pork. A whole pig is cooked

Hong Fa Market is a food lover's landmark in Honolulu's Chinatown.

in a rock-lined oven, called the imu, really a smoky earthen pit. Once the stones are hot, the pig and other dishes are placed in the smoky imu and covered over with earth. Side dishes at a luau might include lau lau (salted butterfish and pork steamed in taro leaves and tied in ti leaves), limu (seaweed), or a mash of poi, created from the ultimate Hawaiian staple, taro. Taro is the root vegetable grown in paddies that sustained the earliest Polynesians; it can be cooked, ground, kneaded into

Hawaiians consume the most SPAM per capita in the US.

flour, or pounded into poi. Poi can be mixed with coconut milk to produce a tropical pudding. Hors d'oeuvres, which are called pupus in Hawaii, are also served at luaus, usually on big platters; wontons, chicken slices, and taro chips are popular pupus, to be shared by the whole table.

Drinks with a Hawaiian touch include cocktails invented to promote the islands in the 1950s (such as the Mai Tai and Blue Hawaiian). The exotic fruit juices in these cocktails are splendid by themselves, especially when served fresh. Even the iced tea has a special flavor in Hawaii (supplied by stirring in fruit syrups). Hawaii also has the only commercially grown coffees in the US. Kona coffee, grown on the hillsides of the Big Island and known for its mellow taste, is one of the world's premier brews. The beans were introduced to Hawaiian plantations in the early 1800s by way of Brazil. Try a cup. Kona coffee will never be fresher or less expensive than it is on these islands.

HANDY TRAVEL TIPS

An A–Z Summary of Practical Information

A

ACCOMMODATIONS

There are hotels for every budget in Hawaii. Major American and international hotel chains are represented on Oahu, Maui, the Big Island, and Kauai. Hotels right on the beach are often the most expensive choice. Rates fall dramatically at hotels a few blocks up from Waikiki Beach in Honolulu, for example, which is the only area where dozens of accommodations options exist. Elsewhere, on all of the neighboring islands, there are clusters of hotels and all-inclusive resorts on or near beaches. Prime resort room rates can easily exceed $400. On the other hand, Hawaiian chains such as Outrigger/Ohana (Tel. (800) OUTRIGGER; <www.outrigger.com>) and Aston (Tel. (800) 92-ASTON; <www.aston-hotels.com>) maintain much lower rates (sometimes less than $100 per night). Smaller local hotels, although they don't offer the services and amenities of major resorts, can be even cheaper (but ask to see rooms, as facilities in the tropics can deteriorate quickly).

Condominiums and vacation homes are common in Hawaii. Overnight rates vary, depending on location and level of luxury, but rates generally fall between those of the small local hotels and the big resorts. Most condo and vacation rentals provide fully-equipped kitchens with modern appliances. Pleasant Hawaiian Holidays (Tel. (800) 242-9244; <www.pleasantholidays.com>, <www.2hawaii.com>) has special packages on many hotels and condos. Bed & Breakfast accommodations are not recommended for budget travelers, since most tend to be luxurious. Bed & Breakfast Hawaii (Tel. (800) 733-1632; <www.bandb-hawaii.com>) handles B&Bs and vacation rentals.

Travel agents, Hawaii package travel services, and travel web sites offer accommodation deals with quite substantial savings. It's best to book accommodations long before arrival, since winter and summer months are busy and conventions sometimes book large blocks of rooms.

AIRPORTS

Honolulu International Airport (Tel. (808) 836-6413) on Oahu, near Pearl Harbor, handles international and inter-island flights at its various terminals, which are connected by free shuttle buses (called Wiki-Wikis). Taxis, hotel shuttle buses, and the island-wide public bus line (TheBus, nos. 19 and 20; Tel. (808) 848-5555) transfer visitors downtown and to Waikiki – about a one-hour ride. No luggage is allowed on TheBus. Many visitors rent a car upon arrival at the airport, but advanced reservations are recommended. The Honolulu Airport is large and busy, with a complete range of services available (stores, restaurants, currency exchange, duty-free outlets). Arrive 2 hours early for international flights, 90 minutes for mainland US flights, and 45 minutes for inter-island flights.

Inter-island flights are frequent. Airport transfers on neighboring islands are limited to taxis, hotel and resort shuttles (hotel reservations required), or self-drive rental cars. Inter-island hops usually take 20–40 minutes.

Maui's main airport, Kahului Airport (Tel. (808) 872-3893), handles some direct flights from the US mainland and many inter-island hops. There's a Visitor Information Center, major rental car counters, and taxi and shuttle stands, but no public transportation. Maui also has two small airports served by a few local airlines, the Kapalua-West Maui Airport (Tel. (808) 669-0255) and the Hana Airport (Tel. (818) 248-8208), which has no regular taxi service.

The Big Island has two airports, Keahole-Kona International Airport (Tel. (808) 329-3423) on the popular west side and Hilo International Airport (Tel. (808) 934-5839) at Hilo. The Keahole-Kona Airport handles most of the traffic, including direct overseas flights from Canada, Japan, and the US mainland, as well as flights from the other islands. There are taxis and rental car counters at both airports, but no public transportation.

On Kauai, the Lihue Airport (Tel. (808) 246-1440) has only one direct flight daily to the US mainland (on United Airlines), but there are numerous inter-island flights from Honolulu and other neighboring island airports. Car rentals and taxis are available. Hoolehua Airport, also called Molokai Airport (Tel. (808) 567-6140) in south-central Molokai, handles inter-island flights only. The same is true at the Lanai Airport (Tel. (808) 565-6757), ten miles from Lanai City. Resort shuttles provide transfers at both Molokai and Lanai. Molokai's airport is served by taxis and car-rental agencies, but there is no public transportation. Lanai has no public buses, either; taxis must be phoned; and rental vehicles must be picked up in Lanai City.

B

BEACH AND OUTDOOR EQUIPMENT

All you need for beach and land activities, from snorkel gear to mountain bikes, can be easily rented at resorts, kiosks on some beaches (such as Waikiki), or specialty shops, such as Snorkel Bob's (<www.snorkelbob.com>). Bob's has outlets on Oahu, Maui, the Big Island, and Kauai, where daily and weekly rates are available.

BUDGETING FOR YOUR TRIP

Prices for almost everything, from groceries to gasoline, are higher in Hawaii than on the US mainland. Neighboring islands can be more expensive than in Honolulu. Budget-minded visitors often pack picnic containers from home; stay at condos with kitchens; buy complete Hawaii packages with bargain rates on flights, accommodations, and rental cars; and avoid the big resorts for equipment rentals and meals. While common necessities are widely available at local stores and shopping centers, these items are worth bringing along, since they can cost 25 to 50 percent more here than at home.

C

CAR RENTAL

Many Honolulu visitors rent a car. The major rental companies have 24-hour counters at most airports. Book in advance for the best deals, and compare offers. See if there will be a drop-off charge; sometimes that can be waived. The collision damage waiver (CDW)

Hawaii

is also optional, but only if its coverage is duplicated by a driver's insurance plan or included when using certain credit cards. With so many rental car agencies in Hawaii, rates can be very competitive, especially weekly rates ($150–200 for economy cars). Convertibles are popular rentals, given the lovely weather, but are more expensive. Gasoline prices are a consideration – they are noticeably higher than on the US mainland. Drivers generally are required to be 25 years of age or older, have a valid driver's license (or International Driving License), and a major credit card. Car rental agencies in Hawaii include Alamo (Tel. (800) 327-9633; <www.goalamo.com>), Avis (Tel. (800) 321-3712; <www.avis.com>), Budget (Tel. (800) 935-6878; <www.budgetrentacar.com>), Dollar (Tel. (800) 800-4000; <www.dollarcar.com>), Enterprise (Tel. (800) 325-8007; <www.pickenterprise.com>), Hertz (Tel. (800) 654-3011; <www.hertz.com>), National (Tel. (800) 227-7368; <www.nationalcar.com>), and Thrifty (Tel. (800) 367-2277; <www.thrifty.com>). Some agencies offer convenient inter-island package deals. Budget, the largest rental car agency in the Islands, offers the widest range of rental vehicles, including many "specialty" cars.

Most highways are paved, but rental companies often list a few remote or unpaved roads where their cars may not be driven. There are fewer car rental agencies and fewer cars to rent on Kauai, Molokai, and Lanai islands, so be sure to book well ahead.

CLIMATE
These tropical islands have fairly uniform, pleasant temperatures year-round. Beaches and lowland areas average about 86°F (30°C) in summer and 77°F (25°C) in winter; low temperatures seldom go much below 65°F (18°C). Cooler average temperatures prevail upland and in the mountains. Sticky weather in summer and rainy, windy days in winter do occur. Tropical storms (July–October) usually stay south of the islands, but hurricanes sometimes hit one or more islands violently (as Hurricane Iniki did on Kauai in 1992). Kauai receives the most rain of the main islands; Hilo on the Big Island is the wettest city in the US; and each island's windward side

(north and east) is wetter and a little cooler than the leeward side. The temperature chart for Honolulu, given below, applies generally to sea-level locations in neighboring islands:

Temperatures	J	F	M	A	M	J	J	A	S	O	N	D
°F		72	72	73	75	77	79	85	85	85	79	77	74
°C		22	22	23	24	25	26	29	29	29	26	25	23
Rain (inches)	4.4	2.5	3.2	1.4	1.0	0.3	0.6	0.8	0.7	1.5	3.0	3.7

CLOTHING

Beachwear sets the tone throughout Hawaii. Bring several swimsuits, shorts, sandals or flip-flops, T-shirts, a long-sleeve shirt, sarong, or other cover-up, a hat, sunglasses, plenty of strong sunscreen, and a water bottle. Off the beach, attire is also informal. Shorts and T-shirts are acceptable wear at most restaurants. For fancier places, long pants (khakis), polo shirts, or sportswear is fine. Aloha wear (Hawaiian shirts, muumuus) is about as formal as it gets; restaurants that require jackets often provide them at the door. A sturdy pair of walking shoes is good for shopping, strolling, and walking on lava; hiking boots may be necessary for difficult trails; and a warm jacket is necessary at high altitudes and crater rims, where temperatures and windchill can approach the freezing mark on any given day.

COMPLAINTS

Report problems in restaurants, hotels, or shops to the respective managers. Hawaii is quite friendly and laid-back. While services may lack efficiency at times, it is easy to discuss shortcomings patiently with those in charge. Direct unresolved conflicts in writing to the Hawaii Visitors & Convention Bureau, Suite 801, 2270 Kalakaua Avenue, Honolulu, HI 96815 (Tel. (800) 464-2924 or (808) 923-1811; <www.gohawaii.com>).

CRIME AND SAFETY

Hawaii is a fairly safe tourist destination, but there are certainly criminals who target tourists. Honolulu is a large city, so avoid walking alone or late at night in its seedier sections. Purse-snatching and pickpocketing do occur on city streets. The most common crime against tourists is directed at rental cars. Lock the doors, leave nothing of value inside, even in the parking lots of popular attractions, resorts, and especially beaches. Thieves can open doors and trunks or smash windows in an eye-blink. Keep valuables under lock-and-key at hotels and safely concealed on your person when shopping and touring. Don't leave purses, pouches, or wallets unconcealed on beaches. In other words, use common sense when traveling on the islands, as you would at any resort destination.

CUSTOMS AND ENTRY REQUIREMENTS

Hawaii is part of the United States, so the customs and entry requirements match those of the US for foreign travelers. All foreign visitors must have a passport (valid for at least 6 months from arrival date) and a visa, obtained from a US consulate. No visas are required for travel to the US for up to 90 days from some countries, including Canada, United Kingdom, Australia, New Zealand, and Singapore. Canadians do not need passports or visas, but evidence of Canadian residency is required. Visitors arriving from the mainland US need not pass through customs or immigration checkpoints. All passengers, arriving or departing, must fill out agricultural inspection forms; passengers from foreign destinations must complete customs declarations. Certain plants, foodstuffs, and all fresh foods and vegetables cannot be taken into Hawaii; some can not be taken back to the US mainland or to foreign countries. Currency or checks exceeding a total of $10,000 must be reported when entering and departing.

D

DRIVING

Driving in Hawaii is much like driving on the US mainland (right side of road). A valid US driver's license, foreign license in English, or International Driving License is required. All passengers must wear seatbelts; infants must be strapped into car seats. Pedestrians, whether in a crosswalk or not, always have the right of way. After a full stop, drivers can turn right from the right lane on a red light if there is no oncoming traffic (unless a sign forbids the turn). Most roads are paved; highways are well-maintained; signs are in English and/or international symbols; speed limits and distance are indicated almost exclusively in miles and miles-per-hour. Gasoline (unleaded only, premium and regular grades) is available at stations (which are mostly self-service); quantities are indicated only in US gallons (one US gallon equals 3.8 liters; one Imperial gallon equals 1.2 US gallons). The American Automobile Association (AAA, Tel. (800) 736-2886; or in Honolulu (808) 593-2221) has reciprocal agreements with some foreign auto clubs. AAA supplies maps, insurance, guide books, emergency road services, and International Driving Permits to its members.

E

ELECTRICITY
The standard US 110-120 volt 60 cycle current is universal in Hawaii. Foreign visitors should bring adapters for appliances, designed to accommodate the regular two flat parallel prongs and the two flat and one rounded prong US configurations.

EMBASSIES/CONSULATES
All embassies are located in the US capital, Washington, D.C. There are consulates in many US mainland cities, including San Francisco and Los Angeles, but in Hawaii there are only the Australian consulate at 1000 Bishop Street, Penthouse Suite, Honolulu HI 96813 (Tel. (808) 524-5050) and the consulate general of Japan at 1742 Nuuanu Avenue, Honolulu, HI 96817 (Tel. (808) 536-2226).

EMERGENCIES
To reach the police, fire department, or an ambulance, dial 911. If you are in a hotel, you can also telephone the front desk, operator, or hotel security.

G

GAY & LESBIAN TRAVELERS

Hawaii is tolerant of homosexual visitors and has active gay and lesbian communities. The Rainbow Handbook Hawaii (Tel. (800) 260-5528; <www.rainbowhandbook.com>) is designed for gay and lesbian travelers. Gay and Lesbian Community Center (Tel. (808) 951-7000) is a valuable information and referral service. The Hawaii Marriage Project (Tel. (808) 944-4598) has updates on the gay-marriage issue. Pacific Ocean Holidays (Tel. (800) 735-6600 or (808) 923-2400) offers gay-friendly vacation packages and lodging options.

GETTING TO HAWAII

Most visitors get to Hawaii on flights from the US mainland. Los Angeles, San Francisco, Portland, and Seattle are the chief west coast gateways; the flight across the Pacific takes 5 to 6 hours. There are some longer, nonstop flights from New York, Dallas, Chicago, and other major cities. United Airlines, American Airlines, Continental Airlines, and Delta Airlines fly to Hawaii, with connections to cities throughout the US mainland. Hawaii's own Hawaiian Airlines (Tel. (800) 367-5320; <www.hawaiianair.com>) and Aloha Airlines (Tel. (800) 367-5250; <www.alohaair.com>) also have direct daily flights from the US west coast to Honolulu, Maui, and the Big Island.

There are also direct flights to Hawaii from Canada using Air Canada, Canadian Airlines, or Canada 3000; from Sydney, Australia, using Qantas; and from Auckland, New Zealand, using Air New Zealand. Hawaii is also served by direct flights from major Japanese, Korean, Taiwanese, Indonesian, and Filipino carriers.

English, Irish, South African, and other visitors across the Atlantic from the US can fly to gateway cities on the mainland on a variety of airlines and then connect to Hawaii using American carriers (which offer very competitive prices to the islands). A visit to New York, Chicago, Dallas, LA, San Francisco, Portland, Seattle, or even Oakland or Las Vegas can be topped off with a fairly quick flight to America's island paradise. Some transatlantic visitors can receive low-priced "Visit America" tickets for discount travel all over the US, including Hawaii, when purchased well in advance overseas.

GUIDES AND TOURS

Guided tours of Oahu are offered by E Noa Tours (Tel. (800) 824-8804 or (808) 591-2561; <www.enoa.com>), with air-conditioned minibuses; Polynesian Adventure Tours (Tel. (808) 833-3000; <www.polyad.com>); and Robert's Hawaii (Tel. (808) 539-9400). Half-day guided tours of Honolulu's Chinatown are conducted on Tuesdays by the Chinese Chamber of Commerce (Tel. (808) 533-3181). Walking tours of Old Waikiki and of other historic neighborhoods in Honolulu are offered by Honolulu Time Walks (Tel: (808) 943-0371). "A Journey to Old Waikiki" walking tour is offered free of charge by Sheraton (Wednesdays, 9–10:30am, Sheraton Waikiki lobby).

Kauai Backroads (Tel. (800) 452-1113 or (808) 245-8809) in Lihue has 4-hour tours of the Garden Island in 4-wheel-drive vans. See where some of over 50 Hollywood films were shot on Kauai in a 5-hour tour by van with Hawaii Movie Tours (Tel. (800)628-8432 or (808) 822-1192; <www.hawaiimovietour.com>). Private off-road tours of Lanai, conducted by Rick Gonsales, are available from Rabaca's Limousine Service (Tel. (808) 565-6670; e-mail rabaca@aloha.net). Ekahi Tours (Tel. (808) 877-9775) uses resident guides for tours of the taro farms in the lush Kahakuloa Valley on Maui.

One romantic way to see Oahu, Maui, the Big Island, and Kauai is to take a whirlwind tour by sea aboard the cruise liners operated by American Hawaii Cruises/United States Line (Tel. (800) 513-5022; <www.cruisehawaii.com>), the only major US-registered cruise operator. These 7-day circle cruises on either the *MS Patriot* from Honolulu or the *SS Independence* from Maui feature Hawaiian arts and entertainment onboard and a choice of top-notch shore excursions at each port; even Hawaiian residents sometimes treat themselves to this cruise. Norwegian Cruise Lines also offers a week-long itinerary with stops at several Hawaiian islands, as well as at one port in the South Pacific.

Hikers can enjoy the guided walks through preserves offered by the Hawaii Chapter of the Sierra Club (Tel. (808) 538-6616; <www.hi.sierraclub.org>) or the Nature Conservancy of Hawaii (Tel. (808) 537-4508; <www.tnc.org/hawaii>).

H

HEALTH & MEDICAL CARE

Although Hawaii has comprehensive medical coverage for most of its residents, visitors are not covered by it. Medical care is expensive, so check your health insurance for coverage while traveling out of state or overseas to Hawaii. Foreign visitors are advised to purchase temporary health insurance to cover overseas travel emergencies. It is wise to travel with prescriptions and medications, although Hawaii has many pharmacies, some open late in the major towns.

The best medical advice for Hawaii visitors is to block out the sun. Wear a hat, sunglasses, and sunscreen at all times. If you are prone to seasickness, use your favorite remedy ahead of time (acupressure band, gingerroot tea, medication). In the water, avoid jellyfish – they can sting. Shark attacks are quite uncommon (less than one attack every two years since 1779). Punctures and cuts (often from coral) should be treated immediately, since there is bacteria in the water.

Hawaii is free of snakes, but the outdoors has three main tropical pests: centipedes, scorpions, and mosquitoes. Scorpions are rare, but their sting requires immediate medical attention; centipedes sting too, and severe reactions mean a trip to the emergency room. Mosquitoes, which arrived by ship at the whaling port of Lahaina in 1826, bite unless repellent is applied first.

HOLIDAYS

The following state and national holidays are observed throughout Hawaii. Banks and government offices are closed on these dates, as are some shops and malls:

1 January	New Year's Day
Third Monday in January	Martin Luther King, Jr. Day

Third Monday in February	Presidents' Day
26 March	Prince Kuhio Day
Last Monday in May	Memorial Day
11 June	King Kamehameha Day
July 4	Independence Day
Third Friday in August	Admission Day
First Monday in September	Labor Day
Second Monday in October	Columbus Day
11 November	Veterans' Day
Fourth Thursday in November	Thanksgiving
25 December	Christmas

L

LANGUAGE

English is spoken by nearly every resident of Hawaii, but the native Hawaiian language, a Polynesian dialect, is undergoing a revival. Visitors are unlikely to hear Hawaiian spoken in the street, but they will see place names and other Hawaiian words posted everywhere. The Hawaiian alphabet consists of seven consonants and five vowels. All words and syllables end in a vowel. Glottal stops are sometimes indicated by apostrophes (an option not employed in this book). Thus, the names of the islands, when pronounced in the Hawaiian way, can sometimes be a syllable longer. Molokai, with 3 syllables, becomes Moloka'i, with 4 syllables; Kauai, 2 syllables, becomes Kaua'i, 3 syllables; Lanai, 2 syllables, becomes Lana'i, 3 syllables. Either pronunciation is acceptable.

Some Hawaiian words have entered common speech on the islands:

alii	Hawaiian royalty
aloha	hello, farewell, love
hale	school
heiau	temple
kahuna	expert, religious leader
kamaaina	resident, local person

Hawaii

kane	man (male)
kapu	forbidden
keiki	child
lomilomi	Hawaiian massage
luau	feast
mahalo	thanks
malihini	newcomer
muumuu	dress, gown
nene	goose (State bird)
ono	delicious
pau hana	end of work day
wahine	woman (female)
wikiwiki	quick

LAUNDRY & DRY CLEANING

Large hotels and resorts usually have laundry and dry cleaning services (expensive); smaller hotels, condos and vacation rentals often offer less expensive washers and dryers. Commercial dry cleaning and laundries abound in most towns, as do self-serve, coin-operated laundromats.

M

MAPS

Hawaii's gift shops and bookstores stock island maps, although they are usually no more detailed than maps sold overseas. The free visitor publications and some rental car company customer magazines provide the most up-to-date road maps.

MEDIA

Hawaii's two daily newspapers, the *Honolulu Advertiser* and the *Honolulu Star-Bulletin*, formerly under the same ownership, have split and gone their separate, competitive ways. Both have timely articles and listings for visitors. Neighboring islands also have their own regional newspapers. *The Honolulu Weekly*, a free "alternative" newspaper, has the most extensive updated listings of what's happening on Oahu. Free tourist magazines (*This Week* and *Spotlight's Gold*) focus on what's available on individual islands. US and international newspapers and magazines are available at bookstores, newsstands, shopping centers, and hotel kiosks, although the selection is far from extensive.

Cable and satellite TV broadcasts, with CNN and other standard US mainland channels, are widely available in hotels and resorts. Local TV stations, affiliated with ABC, CBS, NBC, and Fox, are good sources of US network shows and news; prime-time programs and local news broadcasts are scheduled an hour earlier than in most of the US mainland.

MONEY

Currency: There are bills in denominations of $1, $5, $10, $20, $50, and $100. Higher denominations exist, but are not commonly used. Coins are 1 cent (penny), 5 cents (nickel), 10 cents (dime), and 25 cents (quarter); the 50-cent and $1 coins are seldom encountered.

Currency Exchange: Restaurants and shops rarely accept foreign currencies. Larger hotels, banks in the Honolulu Airport, and currency outlets in the Waikiki area exchange foreign currencies. The best rates are at banks. Neighboring island airports do not provide currency exchange, although some banks and larger hotels do.

Credit Cards: Major cards are widely accepted through the islands at restaurants, hotels, and stores. Car rental agencies require them.

Travelers' checks: In US dollar denominations, travelers' checks are accepted at most stores, restaurants, and hotels.

ATMs: Automated teller machines are everywhere (outside of banks, in shopping malls and grocery stores). The Cirrus network and PLUS system machines work in Hawaii just as they do at home. Be sure you have your PIN number with you when you travel.

O

OPEN HOURS

Museums and tourist attractions have varying hours, but many open about 9:30am; some are closed at least one day a week. Banks have short hours, usually Monday–Friday 8:30am–3pm. Government offices are open Monday–Friday 8am–4pm. In heavily-touristed shopping areas like Waikiki, store hours are generally 9:30am–9pm daily. Shopping centers, malls, department stores, and large groceries have similar long hours, but shops in most towns and cities close about 5:30pm. Restaurants open at 6 or 7am for breakfast, serve lunch from 11:30am–2pm, and begin dinner as early as 5pm. Dinner service usually ends by 10pm; bars, lounges, and nightclubs operate into the wee hours in Honolulu, as late as 4am in Waikiki, but elsewhere even the night spots can close before midnight.

P

POLICE

To report crime or other emergencies, dial 911. Each island has its own efficient, well-trained police force.

POST OFFICES

The US Postal Service (USPS) has numerous offices throughout the islands. Hours vary, but are generally Monday–Friday 8am–4pm, Saturday 8am–noon. Because of Hawaii's remoteness, letters and parcels may take a day or two longer to reach foreign destinations than if mailed from the US mainland. To find the post office nearest you, call (800) 275-8777.

PUBLIC TRANSPORTATION

Honolulu lacks a subway, but it does have TheBus (Tel. (808) 848-5555; <www.thebus.org>), a public transit system that covers much of Oahu (circling the island takes 4.5 hours, but there is no extra cost for distance). There are buses to the airport, to Ala Moana Center, the Polynesian Cultural Center, and to the beaches, from Hanauma Bay to the North Shore. An inexpensive Visitor's Pass (sold at ABC convenience stores) is good for four days of unlimited travel on the system.

Other islands fall far short of Oahu for public transport. The Kauai Bus (Tel. (808) 241-6410) does serve the entire island hourly, stopping at over a dozen coastal towns (but no resorts), but few tourists find it useful for sightseeing. The Big Island's Hele-On Bus (Tel. (808) 961-8744) makes one run each morning from Kailua-Kona to Hilo and one return run each afternoon. Maui, Molokai, and Lanai have no municipal bus or transit service at all.

R

RELIGION

The Hawaiian Islands contain many historic Protestant churches and Catholic cathedrals. Most have active congregations; some have services in Hawaiian as well as in English. Reflecting Hawaii's remarkable patois of races and cultures, visitors will also find a number of historic and still active Buddhist temples. Synagogues and other places of worship are concentrated in Honolulu.

T

TELEPHONE

All of Hawaii uses the 808 area code. The code is not used for intra-island (same island) calls. For inter-island (island-to-island) calls, dial 1, then the area code (808) and the local number. For calls to the US mainland and Canada, dial 1, then the area code and the local number. For international direct dial (IDD) calls from Hawaii, dial 011, then the country code, the area code, and the local number. Calling cards are widely used for long-distance calls; follow the card's instructions.

Note that inter-island calls are charged as long distance calls; that overseas rates, even to the US mainland, are considered high; and that hotels often tack an extra charge on calls you make. The use of international calling cards is the best way to keep charges down. Local calls (on the same island) cost 35 cents from pay phones, but this charge may soon rise (to 50 cents), as it has in some other US states.

TICKETS

Tickets to performing arts and athletic events can be booked by phone and credit card at The Connection (Tel. (808) 545-4000).

Hawaii

TIME ZONES

In Hawaii, situated at -10 hrs GMT, it is two hours earlier than on the west coast of the US mainland in winter, three hours earlier in summer. It is five hours earlier in Hawaii than on the east coast of the US mainland in winter, six hours earlier in summer. (Hawaii does not observe Daylight Savings Time.) Located east of the International Date Line, as are the US mainland and Canada, Hawaii is a day behind Asia and Oceania.

The chart shows the time in winter.

Hawaii	Los Angeles	New York	London	Sydney	Auckland
noon	2pm	5pm	10pm	9am	11am
Sunday	Sunday	Sunday	Sunday	Monday	Monday

TIPPING

Many service employees in the US depend on tips (on which they pay income tax). Customary tips in Hawaii are $1–2 per piece of luggage to bellmen, $1–2 per day to the housekeeping staff, and $1 per trip to parking valets in hotels; $1–2 per piece of luggage to airport skycaps; 10 to 15 percent of the fare to taxi drivers and of the bill to guides; 15 to 20 percent of the bill to the wait staff in restaurants and to hairdressers in salons. Tips are generally not given to other service employees, except in hotels where extra services are sometimes given by doormen and concierges.

TOILETS

Cities and towns in Hawaii seldom have public toilets; beaches and public parks usually do, although they are not always clean. Restaurants, hotels, shopping malls, department stores, and bars usually have clean bathroom facilities, although some of these businesses prefer that you patronize them if using their restrooms. In Hawaiian, kane is the men's side, wahine is the women's side.

TOURIST INFORMATION

For information about all the islands, contact the Hawaii Visitors and Convention Bureau (HVCB), Suite 801, Waikiki Business Plaza, 2270 Kalakaua Avenue, Honolulu, HI 96815 (Tel. (800) GO-

HAWAII or (808) 923 1811; <www.gohawaii.com>). This visitors' bureau also has a mainland branch at 180 Montgomery Street, Suite 2360, San Francisco, CA 94104 (Tel. (800) 353-5846).

The Oahu Visitors Bureau, 1001 Bishop Street, Pauahi Tower, Suite 47, Honolulu, HI 96813 (Tel. (800) OAHU-678, (888) GO-HONOLULU, or (808) 524-0722), has information on Oahu and Honolulu.

The Maui Visitors Bureau, 1727 Wili Pa Loop, Wailuku, HI 96793 (Tel. (800) 525-MAUI or (808) 244-3530), serves visitors to Hana and to East and West Maui.

The Big Island Visitors Bureau runs two branches, one in Hilo at 250 Keawe Street, Hilo, Hi 96720 (Tel. (808) 961-5797) and the other across the island in Kailua-Kona at 75-5719 W. Alii Drive, Kailua-Kona, HI 96740 (Tel. (808) 329-7787).

The Kauai Visitors Bureau, Lihue Plaza, 3016 Umi Street, Lihue, HI 96766 (Tel. (808) 245-3971) has information for travelers to the Garden Isle.

The Molokai Visitors Association, P.O. Box 960, Kaunakakai, HI 96748 (Tel. (800) 800-6367 or (808) 553-3876) is located in the friendly isle's biggest little town.

Lanai visitors can contact Destination Lanai (Tel. (800) 947-4774 or (808) 565-9316) to learn more about this former island plantation.

For information about Hawaii's two National Parks, contact Hawaii Volcanoes National Park, P.O. Box 52, Big Island of Hawaii, HI 96718 (Tel. (808) 985-6000) and Haleakala National Park, P.O. Box 369, Makawao, HI 96768 (Tel. (808) 572-9306).

For information on camping and hiking in Hawaii's state parks, contact the Hawaii State Department of Land and Natural Resources, 1151 Punchbowl Street, No. 130, Honolulu, HI 96813 (Tel. (808) 587-0300).

W

WEB SITES

The Internet provides a plethora of sites for information about Hawaii. Many visitors book accommodations and airfare on-line as well. The sites listed here are the first step in transforming virtual surfers into the real thing:

All of Hawaii: <www.gohawaii.com>
Bed and Breakfast: <www.bestbnb.com>
Big Island of Hawaii: <www.bigisland.org>
Camping and hiking (State Parks): <www.hawaii.gov>
Hawaii Volcanoes National Park: <www.nps.gov/havo>
Haleakala National Park: <www.nps.gov/hale>
Kauai: <www.kauaivisitorsbureau.org>
Lanai: <www.visitlanai.net>
Maui: <www.visitmaui.com>
Molokai: <www.molokai-hawaii.com>
Oahu: <www.visit-oahu.com>
Pearl Harbor USS Arizona Memorial: <www.nps.gov/usar>

WEIGHTS & MEASURES

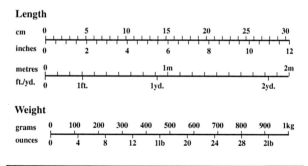

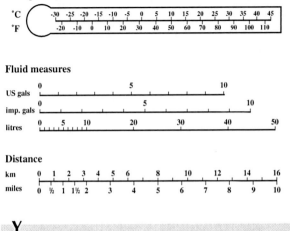

Temperature

Fluid measures

Distance

Y

YOUTH HOSTELS/YMCA

Budget travelers can stay in Honolulu at the Central Branch YMCA, 401 Atkinson Drive, Honolulu, HI 96814 (Tel. (808) 941-3344; fax (808) 941-8821). This YMCA has 114 beds for men only and some doubles open to both sexes. Less expensive are the three youth hostels in Hawaii, two in Honolulu and one on the Big Island at Volcano. Hosteling International Honolulu, located near the University of Hawaii at 2323A Seaview Avenue, Honolulu, HI 96822 (Tel. (808) 946-0591; fax (808) 946-5904), has 43 beds and two private rooms. Hosteling International Waikiki, at 2417 Prince Edward Street, Honolulu, HI 96815 (Tel. (808) 926-8313; fax (808) 922-3798), has 60 beds and 4 private rooms. On the Big Island, Hosteling International Holo Holo Inn, at 19-4036 Kalani Honua Road, P.O. Box 784, Volcano, HI 96785 (Tel. (808) 967-7950; fax (808) 967-8025; <www.enable.org/holoholo/>), has 14 beds and two private rooms.

Recommended Hotels

Accommodations tend to be clustered around popular beaches and other sights in Hawaii. Choices range from expensive all-inclusive resorts and luxury hotel towers to condos, vacation rentals, bed and breakfast inns, and less expensive local hotels. During high season (mid-December–early April), room rates are at their highest. In July and August, vacationers often fill most of the available rooms, so it is important to book ahead (Hawaii's country code is 1; the area code is 808). All accommodations take major credit cards, except where noted. Meals are normally not included, although some hotels and resorts have package specials that include buffet breakfasts.

Each entry is marked with a symbol indicating the approximate room rate charged, per night, for a double room with bath.

$	up to $100
$$	$100–150
$$$	$150–250
$$$$	$250 and more

OAHU

Aston Waikiki Sunset $$$ *229 Paoakalani Avenue, Honolulu, HI 96815; Tel. (808) 922-2700 or (800) 336-5599; fax (808) 922-8785; <www.aston-hotels.com>.* One of Aston's many condominium resort properties, this modern high-rise has large rooms with complete kitchens. Lanais afford views of the Diamond Head end of Waikiki Beach. 410 rooms.

Halekulani $$$$ *2199 Kalia Road, Honolulu, HI 96815; Tel. (808) 923-2311 or (800) 367-2343; fax (808) 926-8004; <www .halekulani.com>.* Very large rooms, most facing the ocean, and luxurious bathrooms with robes, make this a "House Befitting

Heaven," the meaning of its Hawaiian name. With plenty of beachfront, a top French restaurant (La Mer), and the serene House Without A Key outdoor lounge for sunset drinks, Halekulani is a complete resort. 454 rooms.

Hilton Hawaiian Village $$$–$$$$ *2005 Kalia Road, Honolulu, HI 96815; Tel. (808) 949-4321 or (800) 445-8667; fax (808) 947-7898; <www.hawaiianvillage.hilton.com>.* Waikiki's largest resort covers 22 beachfront acres of gardens, lagoons, waterfalls, coconut palms, and swimming pools. There are dozens of shops, a spa, and a branch of the Bishop Museum in the Kalia Tower. Families love this city-within-a-city on the beach. 2,998 rooms.

Hyatt Regency Waikiki $$$–$$$$ *2424 Kalakaua Avenue, Honolulu, HI 96815; Tel. (808) 923-1234 or (800) 233-1234; fax (808) 923-7839; <www.hyattwaikiki.com>.* The Hyatt's two recently-renovated 40-story towers cover a city block at the Diamond Head end of Waikiki's shopping avenue (across the street from the beach). 1,241 rooms.

JW Marriott Ihilani Resort & Spa $$$$ *Ko Olina Resort & Marina, 92-1001Olani Street. Kapolei, HI 96707; Tel. (808) 679-0079 or (800) 626-4446; fax (808) 679-0080; <www.ihilani.com>.* A luxury resort on the west side of Oahu, expertly managed by JW Marriott, Ihilani is situated within a 640-acre resort community that provides golf, tennis, 3 miles of beaches and lagoons, and a world-class spa within a half-hour drive of Honolulu. 387 rooms.

Kahala Mandarin Oriental Hawaii $$$$ *5000 Kahala Avenue, Honolulu, HI 96816; Tel. (808) 739-8888 or (800) 367-2525; fax (808) 739-8800; <www.mandarin-oriental.com/kahala>.* Graceful, elegant, and refurbished for the new century, the venerable Kahala artfully mixes Hawaiian, Asian, and international touches. There's a private beach, swimming pool, and lagoon with resident turtles and dolphins. 402 rooms.

Outrigger Reef $$$ *2169 Kalia Road, Honolulu, HI 96815; Tel. (808) 923-3111 or (800) 462-6262; fax (808) 924-4957; <www.outrigger.com>.* This 17-story tower, perched on one of the best stretches of Waikiki oceanfront, is more deluxe than most Outrigger and related Ohana hotels. Its rooms, views, and amenities rival those of more expensive hotels on the same beach. 883 rooms.

Pacific Beach Hotel $$$ *2490 Kalakaua Avenue, Honolulu, HI 96815; Tel. (808) 922-1233 or (800) 367-6060; fax (808) 922-0129; <www.pacificbeachhotel.com>.* The hotel's twin towers, located at the Diamond Head end of Waikiki, are a block from Kuhio Beach. Rooms have private lanais, refrigerators, and coffeemakers. 830 rooms.

Royal Hawaiian $$$$ *2259 Kalakaua Avenue, Honolulu, HI 96815; Tel. (808) 923-7311 or (800) 325-3535; fax (808) 924-7098; <www.royal-hawaiian.com>.* Waikiki's "Pink Palace," built by the Matson steamship line, has been a landmark since it opened in 1927 on the site of a royal summer palace on the beach. 527 rooms.

Sheraton Moana Surfrider $$$$ *2365 Kalakaua Avenue, Honolulu, HI 96815; Tel. (808) 922-3111 or (800) 325-3535; fax (808) 923-0308; <www.sheraton-moana.com>.* The colonial porte cochère sets the tone for Waikiki's most charming historic hotel, which opened in 1901. The hotel's original Banyan Wing has been restored to its old elegance. The amenities and daily activities are top-notch, as are the buffet meals, especially on Sunday, on the beachfront veranda. 793 rooms.

Sheraton Princess Kaiulani $$$–$$$$ *120 Kaiulani Avenue, Honolulu, HI 96815; Tel. (808) 922-5811 or (800) 325-3535; fax (808) 931-4526; <www.princess-kaiulani.com>.* A block removed from Waikiki Beach, but a few steps from the heart of the Waikiki shopping district, the Princess Kaiulani dates back to 1955, but the rooms are all updated and its 29-story tower is much newer. 1,150 rooms.

Sheraton Waikiki $$$–$$$$ *2255 Kalakaua Avenue, Honolulu, HI 96815; Tel. (808) 922-4422 or (800) 325-3535; fax (808) 923-8785; <www.sheraton-waikiki.com>.* With two 30-story towers, this is largest of Sheraton's four Waikiki beachfront hotels, with the most services and room options. 1,852 rooms.

MAUI

Grand Wailea Resort Hotel & Spa $$$$ *3700 Wailea Alanui, Wailea,, HI 96753; Tel. (808) 875-1234 or (800) 888-6100; fax (808) 874-2411; <www.grandwailea.com>.* Maui's ultimate fantasy resort – said to be the most expensive resort ever built – is a favorite with families. Even has its own seaside chapel for on-site weddings. 780 rooms.

Hotel Hana-Maui $$$$ *Hana Highway, P.O. Box 9, Hana, HI 96713; Tel. (808) 248-8211 or (800) 321-4262; fax (808) 248-7202; <www.hotelhanamaui.com>.* At the end of the legendary road to Hana on Maui's remote and lush east shore, this quiet upscale resort on 66 acres with a wild volcanic oceanfront is the oldest in Maui (1946). The cottages near the shoreline, styled like plantation homes with large covered porches, are luxurious within; some come with private hot tubs. 66 rooms.

Hyatt Regency Maui $$$$ *200 Nohea Kai Drive, Lahaina, HI 96761; Tel. (808) 661-1234 or (800) 233-1234; fax (808) 667-4714; <www.maui.hyatt.com>.* At the south end of the Kaanapali Beach resort complex, the Hyatt Regency is a 40-acre tropical fantasy resort, with exotic birds, waterfalls, garden atriums, and sculpted swimming pools. 806 rooms.

Mauian Hotel on Napili Beach $$ *5441 Lower Honoapiilani Road, Napili Beach, Lahaina, HI 96761; Tel. (808) 669-6205 or (800) 367-5034; fax (808) 669-0129; <www.mauian.com>.* Well north of Kaanapali Beach, the Mauian is a Hawaiian-owned hotel dating back to 1959, restored to its original ambience. All units are equipped with kitchens and ceiling fans (no air-conditioning, TVs, or phones). The free breakfast is a delight. 44 rooms.

Ohana Maui Islander $$ *660 Wainee Street, Lahaina, HI 96761; Tel. (808) 667-9766 or (800) 462-6262; fax (808) 661-3733; <www.ohanahotels.com>.* This is Ohana's first hotel on Maui, equipped with a pool and tennis courts. 360 rooms.

Outrigger Wailea Resort $$$–$$$$ *3700 Wailea Alanui, Wailea, HI 96753; Tel. (808) 879-1922 or (800) OUT-RIGGER; fax (800) 622-4852; <www.outrigger.com>.* This 22-acre oceanfront resort, adjacent to two of the best beaches on the Kona Coast, has a spectacular open lobby and fine rooms with private balconies. 516 rooms.

Ritz-Carlton, Kapalua $$$$ *One Ritz-Carlton Drive, Kapalua, HI 96761; Tel. (808) 669-6200 or (800) 262-8440; fax (808) 665-0026; <www.ritzcarlton.com>.* The most northerly of the western Maui oceanfront resorts, the Ritz-Carlton is a grand hotel with hints of tropical plantation days, set amidst rugged coves and mountains. 548 rooms.

Westin Maui Prince Hotel Makena $$$–$$$$ *5400 Makena Alanui, Kihei, HI 96753; Tel. (808) 874-1111 or (800) 321-6284; fax (808) 879-8763; <www.westin.com>.* The most southwesterly of Maui's big resorts, the Prince has a pretty beach facing Molokini Isle. The rooms are large, lavish, and uncluttered, all with private ocean-view lanais. The courtyard grounds are lush with gardens and immense koi pools. 310 rooms.

BIG ISLAND OF HAWAII

Ohana Keauhou Beach Resort $$–$$$ *78-6740 Alii Drive, Kailua-Kona, HI 96740; Tel. (808) 322-3441 or (800) 462-6262; fax (808) 322-3117; <www.ohanahotels.com>.* This old-fashioned resort from the 1970s has been fully renovated; rooms are sparkling and modern. The grounds, including a royal sacred pool, are lush, and a few steps away is one of the island's best snorkeling and swimming beaches. 311 rooms.

Chalet Kilauea $$–$$$ *P.O. Box 998, Volcano, HI 96785; Tel. (808) 967-7786 or (800) 937-7786; fax (800) 577-1849 or (808) 967-8660; <www.volcano-hawaii.com>.* Brian and Lisha Crawford are the kings of bed & breakfast accommodations in the Volcano area. They have rooms and houses to fit many tastes and budgets, from the lavish to the thrifty. The Chalet Kilauea, the hub of this little empire, serves gourmet breakfasts and afternoon teas. 6 rooms.

Four Seasons Resort Hualalai $$$$ *P.O. Box 1269, Kailua-Kona, HI 96745; Tel. (808) 325-8000 or (888) 336-5662; fax (808) 325-8100; <www.fourseasons.com>.* Upscale bungalows with slate floors, private gardens, and spacious lanais create a relaxing hideaway on the beach. There's a private championship golf course, tennis court complex, and five swimming pools facing the ocean. 243 rooms.

Hilton Waikoloa Village $$$$ *69-425 Waikoloa Beach Drive, Waikoloa, HI 96738; Tel. (808) 886-1234 or (800) HILTONS; fax (808)886-2900; <www.hiltonwaikoloavillage.com>.* A fantasy resort for the whole family, with trams and launches to take guests to their rooms, the Hilton is best known for its swim-with-the-dolphins program. There's also a 1-acre swimming pool with water slides and a vast array of amenities and services all over the 62-acre (25-hectare) oceanfront grounds. 1,240 rooms.

Mauna Kea Beach Hotel $$$$ *62-100 Kaunaoa Drive, Kohala Coast, HI 96743; Tel. (808) 882-7222 or (800) 735-1111; fax (808) 880-3112; <www.maunakeabeachhotel.com>.* Built in 1965 by Laurance Rockefeller, this was the first great resort to be carved out of the lava on the Kohala Coast. It was lauded as the best island resort in the world for years, and it is still one of Hawaii's premier oceanfront resorts, with a vast art collection, a great beach, a major golf course, a loyal staff, and a style all its own. 310 rooms.

Mauna Lani Bay Hotel & Bungalows $$$$ *1400 Mauna Lani Drive, Kohala Coast, HI 96743; Tel. (808) 885-6622 or (800) 367-2323; fax (808) 885-4556; <www.maunalani.com>.* Spacious rooms with lanais face the beach and an atrium complex of gardens and pools in this posh resort, the Mauna Kea's main rival. The shoreline trail leads through ancient fishponds and lagoons where endangered baby sea turtles are raised and released every July 4th. At the end of the trail is a cove and reef where the freed turtles await swimmers and snorkelers. 350 rooms.

Outrigger Waikoloa Beach $$$ *69-275 Waikoloa Beach Drive, Kamuela,, HI 96738; Tel. (808) 886-6789 or (800) 922-5533; fax (808) 886-7852; <www.outrigger.com>.* Renovated in 2000, this full-service resort fronts a tremendous swimming and snorkeling beach with dozens of turtles. 545 rooms.

KAUAI

Hanalei Colony Resort $$–$$$ *5-7130 Kuhio Highway, Hanalei, HI 96714; Tel. (808) 826-6235 or (800) 628-3004; fax (808) 826-9893; <www.marriott.com>.* Nearly at the end of a winding road to the Na Pali Coast, these condominium units are beginning to show their age, but they come with complete kitchens, a white-sand beach with tide pools, and looming mountain peaks out of Bali Hai. No TVs or phones ring out in this paradise. 48 rooms.

Kauai Marriott Resort & Beach Club $$$$ *Kalapaki Beach, Lihue, HI 96766; Tel. (808) 245-5050 or (800) 228-9290; fax (808) 245-5049; <www.hcr.com>.* Hit hard by Hurricaine Iniki, this lavish resort finally reopened, retaining its informal feel, its fine golf courses, its lagoons with exotic animals on the isles, and some of the best hotel pools and swimming beaches in Hawaii. 419 rooms.

Poipu Kapili $$$ *2221 Kapili Road, Koloa, HI 96756; Tel. (808) 742-6449 or (800) 443-7714; fax (808) 742-9162; <www.poipukapili.com>.* These upscale oceanfront condominiums are among the best-maintained on the southern shore. Units are very large, fully equipped (some with washers and dryers). Magnificent sunsets. 60 rooms.

Princeville Resort $$$$ *5520 Kahaku Road, Princeville, HI 96722; Tel. (808) 826-9644; Toll free: (800) 826-1260; fax (808) 826-1166; <www.princeville.com>.* Attractive and luxurious property set on a cliff overlooking Hanalei Bay. Excellent food, wonderful views, great ambiance. Worth the drive. 252 rooms.

Sheraton Kauai Resort $$$$ *2440 Hoonani Road, Koloa, HI 96756; Tel. (808) 742-1661 or (888) 847-0208; fax (808) 923-2023; <www.sheraton-kauai.com>.* An all-inclusive resort on the Poipu shore, Sheraton offers large rooms in three buildings, including two buildings facing a lava rock shoreline. Swimming pools, spa, tennis, and children's programs attract couples and families. 413 rooms.

MOLOKAI

Ke Nani Kai Resort $$ *Kaluakoi Resort, Kaluakoi Road, Maunaloa, HI 96770; Tel. (808) 552-2761 or (800) 888-2791; fax (808) 552-0045; <www.marcresorts.com>.* A family resort on the west side of the island, Ke Nani Kai consists of spacious fully-appointed apartments, a swimming pool, tennis courts, and a golf course. 120 rooms.

Molokai Ranch & Lodge $$$–$$$$ *P.O. Box 259, Maunaloa, HI 96770; Tel. (808) 552-2741 or (877) 726-4656; fax (808) 534-1606; <www.molokai-ranch.com>.* Still a 54,000-acre working cattle and horse ranch on the west side of the island, this is Molokai's most deluxe resort, with fine rooms with large lanais in the new lodge and three clusters of "tentalows" and yurts, including one deluxe camp right on the beach. Outdoor activities run the gamut: horseback riding, ocean kayaking, excellent mountain biking, hiking. 60 tentalows, 20 yurts, 22 lodge rooms.

LANAI

Hotel Lanai $–$$ *828 Lanai Avenue, Lanai City, HI 96793; Tel. (808) 565-7211 or (800) 795-7211; fax (808) 565-6450; <www.onlanai.com>.* A 1923 pineapple plantation guesthouse, this inn near the town square caters to outdoor enthusiasts. Rooms are quaint, with no air-conditioning. Breakfast included. 11 rooms.

Lodge at Koele $$$$ *P.O. Box 310, Lanai City, HI 96793; Tel. (808) 565-7300 or (800) 321-4666; fax (808) 565-4561; <www.lanai-resorts.com>.* Lanai's upcountry, very upscale resort is appointed like an Old English estate, with writing desks, four-poster beds, library, music room. The 21-acre grounds include a croquet court, lawn bowling, horseback-riding stables, formal gardens, and a world-class golf course. 102 rooms.

Manele Bay Hotel $$$$ *P.O. Box 310, Lanai City, HI 96793; Tel. (808) 565-7700 or (800) 321-4666; fax (808) 565-2483; <www.lanai-resorts.com>.* A full-service, quite plush resort on Lanai's finest beach (Hulopoe), the Manele Bay Hotel offers water sports, golf, tennis, a spa, and jeep tours. 250 rooms.

Recommended Restaurants

Hawaii has many excellent dining options both in and outside of the major hotels and resorts, designed to fit all budgets and tastes. Choices range from home-cooked plate lunches to ethnic cuisines reflecting the islands' cultural heritage. Hawaii Regional Cuisine (HRC), using fresh local seafood, fruits, and vegetables and a fusion of Asian, Euro-American, and Polynesian techniques, has put Hawaii on the world map of gourmet cuisines.

Each entry is marked with a symbol indicating the price range, per person, for a dinner comprising appetizer, soup or salad, main course, and dessert. (Drinks, gratuities, and sales tax are not included.) Lunch is generally less expensive than dinner.

$	up to $10
$$	$10–25
$$$	$25–40
$$$$	$40 and more

OAHU (INCLUDING HONOLULU)

3660 On the Rise $$$$ *3660 Waialae Avenue, Honolulu; Tel. (808) 737-1177.* Open Tuesday–Sunday for dinner only. Chef Russell Siu gives Hawaii Regional Cuisine an Asian twist with opakapaka and other local seafood steamed in jasmine tea. Major credit cards.

A Pacific Cafe Oahu $$–$$$$ *Ward Centre, 1200 Ala Moana Blvd., Honolulu; Tel. (808) 593-0035.* Open weekdays for lunch and dinner, weekends for dinner. Chef Jean-Marie Josselin uses local ingredients in a fusion menu, with vegetarian and health-conscious entrées. Major credit cards.

Alan Wong's Restaurant $$$ *1857 South King Street, 5th floor, Honolulu; Tel. (808) 949-2526.* Open daily for dinner only. The chef's creative Pacific Rim fusion menu (ahi cake with grilled eggplant, fresh seafood with lemongrass) is served from an open kitchen in a room with a glassed-in terrace. Major credit cards.

Banyan Veranda $$$–$$$$ *Sheraton Moana Surfrider, 2365 Kalakaua Avenue, Honolulu; Tel. (808) 922-3111.* Open daily for breakfast, lunch, and dinner. Superb gourmet buffets and a sweeping veranda on the beach next to the historic banyan tree make this Waikiki's most romantic spot for an endless Sunday brunch or evening seafood buffet. Major credit cards.

Chef Mavro Restaurant $$$$ *1969 South King Street, Honolulu; Tel. (808) 944-4714.* Open daily for dinner only. Chef George Mavrothalassitis prepares Hawaii Regional Cuisine with a French flair (Provence). Prix-fixe or à la carte. Major credit cards.

Chai's Island Bistro $$ *Aloha Tower Marketplace, 1 Aloha Tower Drive, Honolulu; Tel. (808) 949-2526.* Open daily for dinner, weekdays for lunch and dinner. Chef Chai Chaowasaree is known for fine Thai dishes and Pacific Rim creations. Major credit cards.

David Paul's Diamond Head Grill $$$ *Colony Surf Hotel, 2885 Kalakaua Avenue, Honolulu; Tel. (808) 922-3734.* Open daily for lunch and dinner. Chef David Paul specializes in the New American Cuisine with a Hawaiian flair (Kona coffee-roasted rack of lamb). Major credit cards.

Don Ho's Island Grill $–$$ *Aloha Tower Marketplace, 1 Aloha Tower Drive,, Honolulu; Tel. (808) 528-0807.* Open daily for lunch and dinner. Kitschy, not fancy, this restaurant-museum of Hawaii's most famous entertainer has American and Asian standards, as well as a "surfboard pizza." Major credit cards.

Duke's Canoe Club $$ *Outrigger Waikiki Hotel, 2335 Kalakaua Avenue, Honolulu; Tel. (808) 922-2268.* Open daily for breakfast, lunch, and dinner. Oceanfront alfresco dining on Waikiki beach specializes in the catch-of-the-day and in presenting local musicians. Major credit cards.

Hale Vietnam $–$$ *1140 12th Avenue, Honolulu; Tel. (808) 735-7581.* Open daily for lunch and dinner. Exquisite steaming noodle soups (pho) in this crowded bistro are not to be missed (MSG used). Major credit cards.

Hoku's $$$$ *1Kohala Mandarin Oriental Hotel, 5000 Kohala Avenue, Honolulu; Tel. (808) 739-8780.* Open daily for lunch and dinner. Elegant setting for excellent Asian/European fusion dishes. Major credit cards.

Indigo Eurasian Cuisine $$$ *1121 Nuuanu Avenue, Suite 105, Honolulu; Tel. (808) 521-2900.* Open Tuesday–Friday for lunch and dinner, Saturday for dinner, closed Sunday and Monday. Marvelous Asian-influenced fusion dishes (Buddhist buns, miso-grilled salmon, goat cheese wontons) suit downtown Honolulu's most stylish restaurant. Major credit cards.

Keo's $$–$$$ *2028 Kuhio Avenue, Honolulu; Tel. (808) 951-9355.* Open daily for breakfast, lunch, and dinner. Excellent, long-established, award-winning Thai restaurant uses fresh North Shore herbs and spices. Major credit cards.

La Mer $$$$ *Halekulani Hotel, 2199 Kalia Road, Honolulu; Tel. (808) 923-2311.* Open daily for dinner. Waikiki's most expensive and formal restaurant (jackets required), with a view of Diamond Head, offers superb French dishes prepared by a Michelin-award-winning chef. Major credit cards.

Ono Hawaiian Food $ *726 Kapahulu Avenue, Honolulu; Tel. (808) 737-2275.* Open daily for breakfast, lunch, and dinner. This plate dinner paradise also serves purely Hawaiian dishes (kalua pig, poi, haupia). Major credit cards.

Perry's Smorgy $ *2380 Kuhio Avenue, Honolulu; Tel. (808) 926-0184.* Open daily for breakfast, lunch, and dinner. Inexpensive buffets of basic American and Asian foods, served in a refreshing garden. Second Waikiki location at Coral Seas Hotel on Lewers. Major credit cards.

Roy's Restaurant $$–$$$ *6600 Kalanianaole Highway, Hawaii Kai; Tel. (808) 396-7697.* Open daily for dinner. Chef Roy Yamaguchi's restaurants span the Pacific Rim. This is his flagship eatery, renowned for its fusion of European and Asian cuisines with Hawaiian ingredients. Major credit cards.

Sam Choy's Diamond Head Restaurant $$–$$$$ *449 Kapahulu Avenue, No. 201, Honolulu; Tel. (808) 732-8645.* Open daily for dinner, Sunday brunch. Any restaurant with chef Sam Choy's name is worth trying. Hallmarks are the informal atmosphere, big portions, and creative seafood platters. Major credit cards.

Singha Thai Cuisine $$$ *1910 Ala Moana Blvd., Honolulu; Tel. (808) 941-2898.* Open daily for dinner. An elegant setting for Thai dishes with Pacific Rim variations and local seafood choices, Singha presents Royal Thai dancers nightly. Major credit cards.

MAUI

A Pacific Cafe Maui $$$$ *Azeka Place II, 1279 Kihei Road, Kihei; Tel. (808) 879-0069.* Open daily for dinner. Open kitchen serves up the best of Hawaiian Regional Cuisine from chef Jean-Marie Josselin, with emphasis on local seafood and island meats. Major credit cards.

David Paul's Lahaina Grill $$$$ *127 Lahainaluna Road, Lahaina; Tel. (808) 667-5117.* Open daily for dinner. With a whaling-era bar and an inventive Pacific Rim menu, David Paul's has achieved a top position in Maui dining. Major credit cards.

Haliimaile General Store $$–$$$ *Haliimaile Road, Haliimaile; Tel. (808) 572-2666.* Open daily for dinner, weekdays for lunch, Sunday for brunch. On the way upcountry, this casual restaurant serves superb American-Asian fusion dishes using local ingredients and fresh seafood, the creations of legendary chef Bev Gannon. Major credit cards.

Hula Grill $$–$$$ *Whaler's Village, 2435 Kaanapali Parkway, Kaanapali; Tel. (808) 667-6636.* Open daily for lunch and dinner. Open-air restaurant on the beach features poke rolls and wok-charred ahi for dinner, sandwiches and pizzas for lunch, under chef Peter Merriman, a founder of Hawaiian Regional Cuisine movement. Major credit cards.

Kitada's Kau Kau Korner $ *Makawao; Tel. (808) 572-7241.* Open Monday–Saturday for breakfast and lunch; closed Sunday.

A 50-year upcountry tradition in plate lunches and Hawaiian comfort food that hasn't changed at all. Major credit cards.

Prince Court $$$$ *Maui Prince Hotel, 5400 Makena Alanui, Makena; Tel. (808) 874-1111.* Open Thursday–Monday for dinner, Sunday for brunch, closed Tues, Wed. Elegant dining in southwest Maui with Pacific Rim/Mediterranean fusions for dinner and an elaborate international Sunday brunch with spectacular ocean views. Major credit cards.

Roy's Kahana Bar & Grill $$–$$$ *Kahana Gateway, 4405 Honoapiilani Highway, Kahana; Tel. (808) 669-6999.* Open daily for dinner. Chef Roy Yamaguchi's Euro-Asian fusions featuring the freshest local ingredients and seafood are served up with vigor and flash at the Kahana Bar – and next door, too, at Roy's Nicolina Restaurant. Major credit cards.

Sam Sato's $ *1750 Wili Pa Loop, Wailuku; no phone.* Open Monday–Saturday for breakfast and lunch, closed Sunday. In business since 1933, this very local plate lunch spot, run by the late founder's family, is famous for its "dry mein" dish. No credit cards.

BIG ISLAND OF HAWAII

Batik $$$$ *Mauna Kea Beach Hotel, Kohala Coast; Tel. (808) 882-5810.* Open Sunday–Monday and Wednesday–Friday for dinner only. Dress up (jackets optional) for fine dining featuring Hawaiian Regional Cuisine with a French flair. Major credit cards.

Cafe Pesto $–$$ *Kawaihae Shopping Center, Kohala Coast; Tel. (808) 882-1071.* Open Monday–Saturday for lunch and dinner. Superb pizzas use local ingredients, from blackened ahi to lobsters from the south coast. Also a branch in old downtown Hilo (S. Hata Bldg.). Major credit cards.

Coaste Grille $$$$ *Hapuna Beach Prince Hotel, Kohala Coast; Tel. (808) 880-3192.* Open daily for dinner only. This open-air oceanfront restaurant has wonderful East/West seafood fusions and a fresh oyster bar. Major credit cards.

Huggo's $$$–$$$$ *75-5828 Kahaki Road, Kailua-Kona; Tel. (808) 329-1493.* Open weekdays for lunch, daily for dinner.

Pacific Rim delights and grilled seafood are on the menu, Kailua Bay beach is inches away. Major credit cards.

Keei Cafe $–$$ *Highway 11, South Kona; Tel. (808) 328-8451.* Open Tuesday–Saturday for dinner only. Friendly, affordable, down-home spot using very local ingredients and seafood in eclectic dishes: Hawaiian, Mediterranean, Portuguese. No credit cards.

Merriman's $$–$$$ *Opelu Plaza, Highway 19, Waimea; Tel. (808) 885-6822.* Open weekdays for lunch, daily for dinner. Founding chef Peter Merriman maintains this as the Big Island's premier Hawaiian Regional Cuisine restaurant with fresh local produce, seafood, lamb, and goat cheese. Major credit cards.

Oodles of Noodles $–$$ *Crossroads Shopping Center, 75-1027 Henry Street, Kailua-Kona; Tel. (808) 329-9222.* Open daily for lunch and dinner. Chef Amy Ferguson-Ota offers noodles from around the world, as well as Hawaiian comfort food and East/West fusions. Major credit cards.

Punalu'u Bakeshop $ *Highway 11, Naalehu, South Coast; Tel. (808) 929-7343.* Open daily for breakfast and lunch. Best Hawaiian sweet breads in the islands baked here. Malasadas, sandwiches. No credit cards.

Sam Choy's $$–$$$ *73-5576 Kauhola Street, Kailua-Kona; Tel. (808) 326-1545.* Open daily for breakfast, lunch, Tuesday–Saturday for dinner. Kona's own renowned chef has made this a top family restaurant, with huge servings of Pacific Rim seafood and East/West fusions. Major credit cards.

Sibu Cafe $–$$ *Banyan Court Mall, 75-5695 Alii Drive, Kailua-Kona; Tel. (808) 329-1112.* Open daily for lunch and dinner. With fine Indonesian courtyard décor and Southeast Asian food to match, Sibu has been a local favorite for two decades. No credit cards.

Surt's $$–$$$ *Old Volcano Road, Volcano; Tel. (808) 967-8511.* Open daily for lunch and dinner. This bistro's split menu (European, Asian) has no losers, making it the best dining at the volcano – and the best in downtown Hilo, too, where you'll find Surt's by the Bay (60 Keawe Street; Tel. (808) 969-9601). Major credit cards.

KAUAI

A Pacific Cafe $$$–$$$$ *Kauai Shopping Center, 4-831 Kuhio Highway, Kapaa; Tel. (808) 822-0013.* Open daily for dinner. Chef Jean-Marie Josselin's first restaurant has fine East/West dishes with local ingredients and a Mediterranean flair. Major credit cards.

The Beach House $$–$$$ *5022 Lawai Road, Poipu; Tel. (808) 742-1424.* Open daily for dinner. East meets West in this fine restaurant's fare, with interesting fish and potato variations by chef Jean-Marie Josselin. Major credit cards.

Caffe Coco $–$$ *4-369 Kuhio Highway, Wailua; Tel. (808) 822-7990.* Open Tuesday–Sunday for breakfast, lunch, and dinner. This bistro with a black-light art gallery has affordable gourmet sandwiches and dishes, with emphasis on vegetarian and health-conscious choices. Major credit cards.

Gaylord's $$–$$$ *3-2087 Kaumuali Highway, Lihue; Tel. (808) 245-9593.* Open daily for lunch and dinner; Sunday brunch. Lavish 1930s sugar plantation estate is setting for continental dishes. Major credit cards.

Pacific Bakery & Grill $–$$ *4479 Rice Street, Lihue; Tel. (808) 246-0999.* Open daily for breakfast and lunch, Monday–Saturday for dinner. Affordable, casual Hawaii Regional Cuisine, sandwiches, and pastries, created by chef Jean-Marie Josselin. Major credit cards.

Postcards Cafe $$–$$$ *Kuhio Highway, Hanalei; Tel. (808) 826-1191.* Open daily for breakfast and dinner. Former town museum is the plantation-era setting for Hanalei flapjacks in the morning, gourmet seafood in the evening. Major credit cards.

Tahiti Nui $$–$$$ *Kuhio Highway, Hanalei; Tel. (808) 826-6277.* Open daily for breakfast, lunch, and dinner. Hawaiian family-style dining, with a full luau Wednesday nights. Major credit cards.

MOLOKAI

Maunaloa Dining Room $$–$$$ *Molokai Ranch & Lodge, Maunaloa Village; Tel. (808) 552-0012.* Open daily for breakfast and dinner; Sunday brunch. Molokai's most elegant restaurant uses fresh island greens for salads and catch of the day in a choice of styles (Chinese, Mediterranean, Hawaiian). Major credit cards.

Molokai Pizza Cafe $–$$ *Kahua Center, Wharf Road, Kaunakakai; Tel. (808) 553-3288.* Open daily for lunch and dinner. Lively, friendly family restaurant with Molokai's best pizza and pasta, as well as excellent fish or chicken plate dinner specials. No credit cards.

LANAI

Blue Ginger Cafe $ *409 Seventh Street, Lanai City; Tel. (808) 565-7016.* Open daily for breakfast, lunch, and dinner. Casual, quite local, this pleasant café serves plate lunch fare, often with a Filipino twist. No credit cards.

Formal Dining Room $$$$ *Lodge at Koele, Lanai City; Tel. (808) 565-4580.* Open daily for dinner only. Award-winning gourmet American cuisine, served in an English manor (jackets required), includes island venison and fresh seafood. The more casual Terrace next door serves fine American fare all day. Major credit cards.

Henry Clay's Rotisserie $–$$ *Hotel Lanai, 828 Lanai Avenue; Tel. (808) 565-7211.* Open daily for dinner. American country cuisine, using fresh seafood, produce, and game, is served in the town's historic plantation inn. Major credit cards.

Ihilani $$$$ *Manele Bay Hotel; Tel. (808) 565-2290.* Open daily for dinner. Elegant ocean-view dining room is a formal setting for gourmet Mediterranean and French creations, with local Hawaiian ingredients added. Hawaiian Regional Cuisine is the focus of the hotel's other top, more affordable restaurant, Hulopoe Court. Major credit cards.

Pele's Other Garden $ *Dole Park Square, Lanai City; Tel. (808) 565-9628.* Open Monday–Saturday for lunch and dinner. Excellent New York-style deli fare, fresh and organic. Major credit cards.

INDEX